CHILDHOOD

A Young Girl's Experiences During World War II

Eva Kamm Romano

WESTCOM PRESS

New York   Los Angeles   Washington DC

Westcom Press
2101 N Street, NW
Suite T-1
Washington, DC 20037

westcomassociates@mac.com

18 17 16 15 14 13 12 11 1 2 3 4 5

ISBN - Hard Cover: 978-0-9665827-6-5

ISBN - Soft Cover: 978-0-9665827-9-6

Library of Congress Number: 2011924982

In loving memory of my parents
Irena and Josef Kamm

Preface

Transcribed from incomplete sentences and single words written on scraps of paper, this memoir conveys neither the depth of fear and horror I experienced in the years 1939–1942 nor the desolation and loneliness I felt after the final separation from my parents in 1942, after Hitler and his armies had swept across Poland, leaving it free of Jews. My abbreviated notes did not include details, no minutiae. Sometimes a single word was a reminder of a whole happening, and my story may lack dimension because of this.

The greatest trouble I had when transcribing my notes was not being able to describe my family members better. My time with them was so short that I did not really know them.

I had difficulty starting this memoir, perhaps for no other reason than the volume of work it presented. But I felt deeply that I had to organize and arrange in order the notes that I had made during the war.

When I look back over those years, I draw from my childhood as if from a life-giving well. Brutal as that time was, it is a source of great emotional comfort to me. My close-knit family; adoring parents and grandparents; the small, beautiful town where we lived; a complete sense of belonging—all offer strength and solace. Many of my memories are painful; yet they often serve as an escape from a difficult and sometimes unbearable reality. I read somewhere, "I think that one recollection from youth can sometimes keep a man from suicide, lead him away from hopelessness and despair." I agree with the author of those words.

Childhood

By my thirteenth birthday, I had lost my parents, other immediate and distant family members, my home, and my identity. Confused, I watched with resignation the terrible cruelty of which people are capable. I thought that hiding to avoid being killed would be my lot in life.

Now that I have written down everything, I am able to destroy the scraps of paper that have helped me hold onto my past (and that in themselves gave pain), scraps and pages covered in the childish handwriting of two languages, neither of which I use today. I hope finally to have freed myself to the point where I will be able to speak about my childhood—something I could not do for fifty years.

Having been defrauded of everything that is basic in life, I saw the memories of my childhood as a precious personal possession, and to speak about them freely over the years would have lessened their importance. It might have lightened the burden, but it would have diminished the treasure.

Sharon, Connecticut, August 27, 1997

Katowice

One

"Katowice," Mother said, planting a seed in Father's head and then cultivating it until the move was made from our small town of Dabrowa. She had dreamed of being assimilated into a more cosmopolitan way of life than the one she was used to, and she knew that this was not possible living in Dabrowa, near her parents, where cultural outlets were few.

Katowice, Upper Silesia, Poland, is an industrial area rich in minerals: coal, iron, lead. But that was not what attracted Mother. She was drawn to the place because Upper Silesia did not have a purely Polish atmosphere. It had for many centuries been occupied by Prussia, and Germans had moved to that area over long periods. In the late 1870s, when Prussia incorporated Upper Silesia into the Third Reich, more Germans arrived, merging with the native Polish population. In 1919, at the Treaty of Versailles, Upper Silesia was given back the Prussian sector, which once more became Poland. Mother liked the idea of using more than one language— she was fluent in German—and the busy place of Katowice, where German was spoken with the same frequency as Polish, was far more appealing than her sleepy little hometown.

Our apartment in Katowice was on the third floor in a five-story building that ran the length of a quiet block on Gliwicka Street. The exterior of the building was gray stucco-covered brick. On either side of this long structure rose a column of balconies, gay in summer with geraniums and other seasonal flowers. Gliwicka Street was residential. Apartment buildings in various shades of gray lined both sides of the street. Three stores dotted the several blocks that composed the neighborhood: a dry cleaner; a delicatessen, featuring imported canned food; and a bakery I remember particularly well because it was located in the basement of our building. Adding cheer to the neighborhood was the park at the north end of the block, Plac Wolnosci (Freedom Park), where I spent many hours in happy play.

Our apartment consisted of several large, sunny rooms, all of which faced the street, where yellow tramways and an occasional automobile passed. Each wallpapered room had a highly polished red floor, even the kitchen. Periodically, the floors were waxed and polished, and at those times, I was not allowed to mar their beauty by stepping on them: instead I was told to walk on the rugs. Oriental rugs were scattered throughout the apartment, and the furniture was what my parents considered modern and what years later would be referred to as Art Deco.

The bedrooms were heated by floor-to-ceiling ceramic tile stoves, fueled with coal. In winter my down coverlet was held up against the stove for a few minutes to warm it before I got into bed.

Surrounded by the coalfields of Upper Silesia, Katowice was perennially dusted with sooty grit. Clothing and bed linen had to be changed frequently; furniture was polished daily; and for an unobstructed view, windows were continually being cleaned.

In addition to a live-in maid and kinderfraulein (nanny), we had two laundresses come once a month to wash enormous amounts of laundry. A communal laundry room was located in the attic of the apartment building, and I loved visiting there when the laundresses were at work. Just getting to the room was an adventure. First, I climbed two flights of stairs to the fifth floor, then another half flight to the dark, barren attic, which had to be crossed half the length of the entire building, its floorboards creaking with each step. In that gloom, I imagined ghosts hiding behind beams in dark corners. Momentary panic would make me stop to listen for strange moans or sighs before hurrying on.

The laundry room, bright with electric bulbs hanging from the ceiling, was full of steam, smelling of soap. Laundry boiled in big vats over huge fires built in brick fireplaces, while the laundresses, their faces pouring sweat, fiercely rubbed sheets against washboards, soap oozing all over. My entrance would instantly stop all work. "Look who is here," they would call out. Then crouching to face me, they would ask questions, stroking my hair.

I also liked visiting neighbors in winter, when it was too cold to play in the park. Most were adults because few children lived in our part of the apartment house. Being an only child, I sought company regardless of age or gender. A special favorite was a wealthy bachelor who lived directly below us with his housekeeper, Anna. Of course, he was rarely home when I visited, but Anna always made me feel welcome, especially when her little nephew visited. He and I would have the run of that antiques-filled home. We liked playing house under the dining room table: there, on a thick Persian rug, I set up my doll furniture and played mother. One day the boy kissed my cheek, saying that all fathers kissed mothers. I was embarrassed, but I liked it.

My father commuted daily to Sosnowiec, a textile center where he owned a factory, making woolen knits. His life seemed fully absorbed by his business. He left early each morning and came back late at night. On those rare occasions when he was home early enough for us to take the evening meal together, I would jump on his lap with a book and beg for a story before bedtime; he never refused, reading for as long as it took me to fall asleep in his lap.

Mother's household ran by the clock—everything at its appointed time. Dinner was served at one o'clock, and by two-thirty, Nanny and I were in the park while Mother napped. At four, Mother took tea with her friends at Martyka's, a popular coffeehouse in

Katowice, and we ate a light supper at six. Bedtime for me was at seven. We followed that schedule until World War II broke out in 1939, when I was allowed to stay up later; and when the war began affecting each of us directly, none of mother's schedules could be followed. I felt relieved not to be so regimented, but I also felt the loss of a comfortable life with all its predictability. And I was saddened to see Mother giving up. It meant so much to her to have a well-ordered life.

In Katowice I rarely played with more than one or two other children. At that early age, I had no special friend. I was considered introverted. I invented games for myself, made little people and toys out of fallen horse chestnuts and toothpicks, and engaged Nanny in my diversions. I also liked playing with sand, examining each grain for its color and shape. I saw a new world in the diversity of the grains. Those musings freed me from the restricting atmosphere of home, parents, maids. At night, before falling asleep, I would bury my face in the pillow and see millions of gold stars against a dark night, swaying from one direction to another in slow motion.

I played with dolls and other toys only with other children because it was their choice. Sometimes I hung over the balcony railing, stretching to catch a glimpse of the park; then a pair of arms would lift me off the railing and deposit a resounding slap across my bottom. "How many times do I have to remind you not to hang on the balcony railing?" Mother would glare down at me as she closed the French doors. I could not have heard her sneaking up behind me. Afraid she might frighten me and cause me to fall over the railing, she would stretch her long legs, soundlessly like a cat, across the room, catching hold of me before I had a chance to move.

An only child, thin and often ill with colds, I was doted on by my parents and the rest of the family, probably because I was born exactly one year after my sister died of leukemia at age nine. Fearing constantly for my health and well-being, my parents often took me to doctors for checkups and on vacations for a change of air to improve my appetite.

Doctor Sachs, the pediatrician, discovered that I was anemic, and she prescribed as a daily addition to my diet a quarter pound of ham sprinkled with the juice of half a lemon. This was a difficult cure to follow at home because mother kept a kosher house, and ham is not a kosher food. Therefore, each afternoon, regardless of the weather, while Mother had tea, the maid and I walked to the pork butcher's, where I had my "medicine." This turned out to be the only meal in the day I really enjoyed.

Delicate and sensitive, I would weep when I heard a sad story and would stay downcast for long periods. That sadness often turned to fear—a fear I could not explain. Mother kept asking, "What do you fear?" to which my only answer was "I don't know." I could not put into words what that feeling was. It was usually a foreboding, an anticipation of some impending catastrophe, and for a long time, the only remedy that helped was gypsies. Groups of gypsies often invaded our courtyard and performed for hours, playing the accordion and singing while their children danced and performed acrobatics. Sometimes, only a young couple would come, the man playing a violin while the woman sang melancholy songs in a plaintive voice. I preferred the family groups with children who danced. During the shows, people who hung out their windows watching and applauding would drop coins wrapped in paper down to the performers. This kind of entertainment gave me courage not to be afraid because it offered a glimpse of life so different from mine, a life that was precarious, even dangerous, I thought.

* * *

One fall afternoon when I was about five years old, on the way back from the pork butcher, Nanny decided to take the long way home. We strolled slowly and made occasional comments about how quickly the clouds moved in and covered the sun. Suddenly, a deafening thunderclap interrupted us. Afraid of being caught in the storm, Nanny rushed through the streets, dragging me behind her.

Huge splashes of rain marked the sidewalks as we ran over them, she a step ahead, pulling me by the hand. We were crossing a street when a motorcycle appeared out of nowhere, furiously rounding the corner. Nanny was already on the sidewalk, but I had to take another step and at that moment was hit by the motorcycle and thrown against the curb. I did not lose consciousness, but I lost all my upper and lower front teeth. Nanny screamed, and I sat on the sidewalk weeping.

The driver parked his motorcycle and came over to me. "Don't cry, little girl. Mommy will give you a bath and you'll be fine. Don't cry," he murmured, "you will soon feel better, and you will get your second teeth."

"But that will be a long time from now," I tried to say, but the flow of blood, lack of teeth, and my swelling mouth would not allow me to speak.

Meanwhile, a few people had gathered around us, talking all at once, blaming the rider of the motorcycle for his negligence while he apologized to all. In the commotion, he took a ten-zloty bill from his wallet, handed it to Nanny, then, wishing her good luck, jumped on his motorcycle and took off with a roar.

A man from a nearby candy store brought a damp cloth to stem the flow of blood. Nanny picked me up off the sidewalk, holding the cloth to my face, and carried me into the candy store, where she spent the ten zloty on an enormous box of chocolates. After a while, she lifted me off the counter, piled her purchase on top of me, and started home. "What will I say to your mother?" Nanny wailed, while drops of blood collected on my lap and on the box of candy. I stared at her, unable to make sense of things.

Walking up the stairs at home, we caught up with Mother, who was returning from afternoon tea. She stopped in her tracks, as if unable to move. Mother made no sound as she took me out of the woman's arms while listening to her confusing account of what had happened. She unlocked the door and asked Nanny to prepare my bed and run the tub. When I was comfortably settled, Mother dialed the pediatrician and, asking Nanny to take the chocolates with her, discharged her. Nanny could not leave fast enough.

During the recovery period after the accident, I asked for a pound of coffee beans because I wanted to count. Making groups of ten, I was left with one odd bean. Not knowing what to do with it, I decided to hide it in my right nostril. I pushed it up so high that it caused me to scream in pain, which brought Mother to my bedside. When she discovered what had happened, she quickly wrapped me in blankets and took me to the doctor. Sitting in the waiting room, Mother worked on my nose. Holding my left nostril tightly, she instructed me to "blow hard" while pressing the upper part of the right nostril. Other waiting patients cheered me on, and before our turn came to see the doctor, the bean popped out, falling noiselessly to the carpeted floor.

Very soon after this, we got new help; her name was Bronia. She had thin light brown hair, which she wore shoulder length, and the skin on her face was pockmarked. When Father saw her, he said, "She is built like a prize fighter."

Before Bronia, Mother had tried various nannies. She longed for a life where Polish culture played a greater role than did Jewish culture. She especially wanted me to grow up unhampered by religion. I remember nannies who were born in France, hired on the chance that I would learn some French; nannies who were part-time students, employed so that they could talk with me about their studies; and nannies hailing from different parts of the country—even from as far away as Russia—to familiarize me with their backgrounds, broaden my way of looking at things, and dilute somewhat the strictly religious way of life we observed in our home, which my mother felt obligated to observe because of her orthodox upbringing. All the personalities who passed through our household, their philosophies and their religious training, their attitudes and values, shaped my outlook on life to some degree. But my parents' moral standards together with their strong sense of family values influenced me most.

I never developed any close relationships with the women who took care of me except with Bronia, whom I loved and who loved me in return. I vividly remember our walks, during which she filled my head with various aspects of the Christian religion. She would take me to church at Easter to show me the laid-out figure of a bisque Christ bedecked with flowers, a wreath of thorns on His head. At other times, when she was in a less pious frame of mind, she spoke dirty words I did not understand and never repeated at home, knowing them instinctively to be "bad." I treated that as our secret.

Bringing me home from various outings, Bronia needed only to look at me to know if all was well. Was I happy to be back home? Was something bothering me, something perhaps that we saw on our walk? She was also happy to help me eat my food. I had a small appetite, and Bronia knew that I suffered when Mother made my plate. So, volunteering to "feed" me, she would eat part of my food, making me happy and helping to avoid a crisis at nearly every meal. Years later, it occurred to me that she needed more food than she was given by Mother. But food was plentiful in our house, and Mother was generous with it.

Bronia was a good friend, and I considered her help another of our secrets. Mother never found out what Bronia was teaching me. If Bronia had been let go, I would have been extremely unhappy, even though after I grew up and thought of her, I saw that honesty was not what I was learning.

Rude or brutal events or stories brought back my unknown demons, intensifying that vague fear I so often felt. Stories in which offspring were abandoned or abused frightened me. My fears might perhaps have been best defined as worry about being left alone, orphaned. Often during a sleepless night, I would climb into my parents' bed, lying between them for comfort and reassurance. Then, feeling protected, I would sleep.

Mother read stories to us before bedtime, stories with happy endings. I had favorite fairytales, and I particularly liked stories of animals and insects and their adventures. With Mother reading and Bronia listening with me, I would keep my ears tuned to Mother's voice and my eyes resting on Bronia until sleep came.

Two

At home we spoke Polish, but Mother and Father often lapsed into Yiddish. I did not speak it, nor did I understand it. We observed all Jewish holidays, and no one but Mother cooked. She feared that a hired cook would not follow the orthodox dietary laws. Mother always sang when she cooked, and later, coming home from school, I would hear her beautiful soprano singing a Puccini aria or a currently popular Polish song as I climbed the stairs.

Although Mother enjoyed the bourgeois life, she used restraint in everything she did, keeping an eye on the bills and handling all food preparations when she entertained at small dinners or teas. She developed certain recipes for which she became famous among her small circle of friends.

The synagogue to which we belonged—a round, red brick, Romanesque-style building—was orthodox. Houses of worship for different Jewish denominations, such as Conservative or Reform, as there are in America today, did not exist in Poland, at least not in my recollection. (Conservative preserves the essential elements of traditional Judaism but allows for the modernization of religious practices, and Reform does not adhere to many traditional beliefs.) That's not to say that all Jews in Poland were orthodox. Particularly in Katowice, those who practiced their religion did so mostly by eating kosher food in their homes and by attending synagogue on holidays. At other times, their lives seemed unaffected by special religious restrictions. I don't remember ever seeing Jews in traditional orthodox garb in Katowice. In small towns, however, orthodox Jews lived in isolated areas, self-imposed ghettos, where life had not changed in hundreds of years. There one saw the Hasidim and their families practicing Talmudic Judaism.

* * *

My parents' marriage was not a happy one. When I got older, I found out that Mother had married because she had passed her twentieth birthday (old at that time), and Father, who was eleven years older, had pressed her to marry him. More pressure came from Grandmother (mother's mother), who could not understand anyone not wanting to marry when the opportunity was there. Mother's hesitation stemmed from reasons that were invalid to my grandmother. Mother had a formal education, having finished gymnasium; Father did not. Her tastes were those of an intellectual: lectures, books, the opera. His life comprised his business and his family. Father loved horses, having grown up in a home where all the males were horse traders, starting with his grandfather and followed by Father's two brothers. Mother knew nothing about horses, nor was she interested in them.

I perceived my parents' separateness, and I loved them separately, but the atmosphere was somehow disturbed when they were together. They didn't fight, but conversation was generally minimal and impersonal, and the love I had for them was tinged with pain as I discerned them to be unsuited.

I always tried to please Mother because I felt confident with her choices—I knew them to be right. I also knew that she was reliable, that I could depend on her for everything, and that if I followed her example, I could not go wrong. Ever since I can remember, I have measured my accomplishments by her standards; indeed, I do so to this day.

She was tall and elegant. Her salt and pepper hair was parted in the middle and combed into a page boy, highlighting dark green eyes, high cheekbones, a fine straight nose, and a brilliant smile—that was

Mother, Irena (Ita) Kamm. Some people said that she looked like Greta Garbo. What did that matter? Most important for me was that she knew the answers to my questions. I was proud of her.

Mother belonged to various political organizations. Her interests were in worldwide politics as well as in the politics of Poland and how these politics affected Jews. She was a voracious reader, reading three newspapers daily: the Polish, the Yiddish, and the German. She spent great amounts of time by herself, busy with her world. Stacks of books cluttered her night table, waiting to be read. She belonged to book clubs, where she recommended titles and led discussions. One could ask her any number of questions concerning literature, poetry—classical or contemporary—history, or current events and she gladly stopped what she was doing to explain and explain again if it wasn't clear, a charming smile lighting up her face when the listener showed understanding. How often did I ask questions that led to those lucid, thorough answers, leading to further questions and ending finally with her smile? Mother loved the Polish language, and she tried to instill that love in me. She wanted me to speak it fluently, with eloquence, the way she did. From her, I inherited a love of reading and a great need for solitude.

Mother was not a tolerant woman. She expected me to behave well and listen to her instructions at all times. She expected good service and appropriate behavior from the servants. She was the eldest of three sisters and one brother, all of whom now lived in Katowice, and all of whom were periodically criticized or reprimanded by her for one thing or another.

Mother was disappointed in Aunt Franka, the middle sister, because she was unaware of current political news. Aunt Gusta, the youngest sister, was criticized for the dowdy clothes she wore or because her children were not disciplined. Uncle Herman was scolded for gambling and womanizing. Since he was the youngest,

Josef Kamm, World War I

Mother felt an obligation to guide him and to point out his mistakes. Unfortunately, he paid no attention to her, which caused her severe anguish.

Father, too, came in for his share of criticism. He was, for instance, not allowed to burp at the table or to lift the dessert saucer to his mouth. "There are spoons for this," she would say sternly. But he managed to get around her by saying, "Let me show you how we ate when I was in China," whereupon he would pick up the dessert dish—usually containing softly stewed fruit—and slurp it down noisily while grinning broadly.

Mother was intolerant of noise, dirt, foolish chatter, bad taste (such as talking loudly in public places), and being aggressive or demanding. She also had difficulty admitting when she was wrong. I remember taking English lessons shortly before World War II. Twice weekly, a teacher came to our apartment to instruct us. At that time, my parents began to talk about emigrating to the United States. Aunt Franka and her husband were to join us in America, so they also attended the lessons.

Uncle Herman joined our group because he was curious and adventurous.

Mother had some difficulty with the pronunciation of the *w*, giving it the hard "v" sound, and I tried to correct her, but she simply did not hear the difference in the two sounds. She was so adamant about this that I stopped correcting her. All this made her quite unhappy, and I was afraid that anger would follow. At that point in my life, I never feared anything quite as much as I feared mother's anger.

When Mother got angry, it was Götterdämmerung—like an erupting volcano. Her face would redden as she shrilly spewed angry words, threatening punishment. A few slaps across my bottom were not beneath her at those times. Imprisoned by her upbringing and the times in which she lived, frustrated by her circumstances, this gifted woman was sometimes brought to vent her anger on a child.

Even then, as young as I was, I thought of how the measure of her outbursts was out of proportion to my misbehavior. I don't think she was fully aware of why she got as angry as she did. She was not subservient to my father, but in so many other areas of her life, she simply had to be passive. Her good mind and her broad knowledge probably only frustrated her because there was never a question of Mother going to work outside the home— none of the women in our family worked at that time. She had no satisfactory outlet for her talents, so every once in a while, she erupted like a volcano, using any small pretext to get rid of pent-up energy and frustration.

On one occasion, Uncle Herman was making fun of her pronunciation, and a loud exchange passed between them. The lesson was over, and the teacher left. Aunt Franka, Uncle Emil, and I looked on. "Sala, didn't we work together on this?" Mother shouted. I remained silent. Uncle Herman laughed, saying, "Sala, tell

Sala Kamm Age 6

your mother to listen to the rest of us pronouncing the *w* and ask her if it sounds the same as her pronunciation." He then turned to the door. Mother crumpled a sheet of newspaper and threw it at him as he closed the door behind him.

I don't remember ever being hugged by Mother, but that was not from a lack of love—her actions proved her love daily. Mother's family was not demonstrative; no one showed their love openly. Neither her sisters nor my grandmother was sentimental—they were realists. Yet Mother was nurturing in her unique way by being patient and by showing how proud she was of me when I did something well. She used all her varied knowledge to raise me to be a self-reliant, capable person.

Father made up for Mother's lack of affection. I had wonderful times with my father in different ways than those with my mother. We would spend money together—he bought whatever I pointed to. Mother frowned on those outings and accused Father of spoiling me, but he just laughed. He had no deep knowledge of literature or poetry. He knew some history, and he knew the history of the Jewish people. His knowledge was of the land, of plants and of animals, particularly horses, having been brought up around them.

Grandfather Kamm, Father's father, traded in horses, and later his youngest son, my uncle Meyer, earned his living the same way. Living in Katowice, Father had no opportunity to be around and enjoy any of the things he knew and loved, so his sole interest was his business in Sosnowiec, a commercial textile center near Katowice. He was frequently away from home for several days at a time, but when he returned after these absences, I would happily sit on his lap and have him read to me.

I loved my father as much as I loved my mother, but for different reasons; he was quiet, kind, and very affectionate. I could ply him with questions and demand attention in many different ways; even when he was tired, he never protested, never refused. I could ask for whatever came to my mind, and it would not occur to him to say no. He helped friends and strangers for the asking, and I always saw him giving alms to beggars on our excursions.

Blond, with almond-shaped blue eyes, he was shorter than Mother, and possibly because of this difference in height, they never walked together, one always either a few feet behind the other or separated by half a block, while I ran from one to the other, now holding hands with her, and a few moments later, holding on to him, Josef (Joske) Kamm, my father.

Sometimes on these walks, Mother would say, "Let's stop at Martyka's," and once in a while Father would say, "Let's play the lottery; let Sala pick the numbers," to which Mother would respond, "I'll wait outside." I learned early in life that my money would not come from playing the lottery. At other times, the three of us would walk across town to a fancy specialty shop where you could find fresh tomatoes in winter and layer cakes with fresh orange sections arranged on top. I don't remember which of all these places I liked best, but I remember loving fresh tomatoes in winter.

Twice each year, at the change of seasons, Mother would ask Father to bring from Sosnowiec (a mecca for textiles) various fabrics—silks, woolens, cottons—for dresses, suits, and coats for me and for herself. Then a seamstress for dresses and a tailor for coats and suits would come to the house to discuss styles and take measurements. I owned countless dresses, coats, shoes, leggings, and other accessories for matching outfits. Mother loved beautiful clothes. She picked the materials for Father's suits with as much care as she did for her own clothes. It would take weeks of measuring, trying on, changing, and adjusting until the clothes were delivered ready for wear.

* * *

For some time Father had been complaining about having to commute between Sosnowiec and Katowice, and before my seventh birthday, when I would officially start school, all three of us went to Sosnowiec to look for an apartment with the thought of moving there so that Father could be close to his business.

Sosnowiec was physically very different from Katowice. The streets were narrower, and the sidewalks were uneven. One end of a sidewalk would be high, where one had to take a long step down onto the curb, while the other end met the curb evenly. In general, the town seemed neglected, not as clean or as well taken care of as Katowice. Mother noticed these things immediately. But the apartment we looked at was large, with many sunny rooms, and it would have been more comfortable than the one we had in Katowice.

At first the decision seemed easy—we would move. But when Mother found that schools for Jewish children in Sosnowiec were inferior to those in Katowice, both parents agreed to remain in Katowice. The discussion of that apartment continued for weeks, and I regretted not being able to live in it, but my parents had made up their minds, and as was usual for him, Father good-naturedly accepted the inconvenience of traveling to work.

I heard many of my parents' conversations before falling asleep. These usually had to do with vacation plans, upcoming holidays, Father's business, or politics. They often disagreed, but I never heard them fight, and until World War II broke out, I never heard any discussions about money. In 1939, these discussions took a different turn. We would emigrate to America. Father's eldest sister lived in North Carolina, and in her letters, she began to urge Father to leave Poland.

There was a lot to consider: Father had a well-established business, Mother had her friends, and I was about to enter school. What I now heard in my parents' conversations was a tug of war.

Mother: "We will be in a strange country without friends, without the language."

Father: "We would have Dora and her family. And you, Irena, with your knowledge of politics and all the papers you read, should know better than anyone that what the papers say sounds ominous, especially for the Jews. I don't want to leave Poland any more than you do—we have a good life here."

Mother: "Then why are we even talking about this?"

"Because the safety of my family is more important than a business," Father responded.

"Can we bring Bronia?" I piped up.

Three

Two of Father's siblings owned hotels in Krynica, a popular summer resort in Poland. Aunt Raisa, one of Father's sisters, had a large and luxurious hotel that was famous for its fine cuisine and particularly for its bakery. Uncle Meyer's wife ran a much smaller establishment, presiding over the kitchen herself. Both families maintained homes in Dabrowa, where they moved after the summer season, Aunt Raisa with her family to rest and Uncle Meyer to trade in horses while his wife rested, preparing for another busy summer.

Every June Mother and I traveled to Krynica, where she took the waters. She stayed under a doctor's care on a six-week cure of mineral waters for nerves and stomach disorders. Those vacations consisted of eating, sleeping, and changing clothes. We alternated staying at Aunt Raisa's one year, then Uncle Meyer's the next.

I preferred staying at Uncle Meyer's because there I could play with my two cousins Leon and Ceska, Uncle's children. Together we explored the countryside near the hotel. I felt safe and relaxed in their company. I also discovered in myself a predilection for adventure, much to Mother's consternation. With Ceska and Leon I climbed hills, looked for strange insects, and caught baby frogs and butterflies. My cousins were slightly older than I, and since Krynica had been their summer home for years, they knew the best places to explore and were quite adept at setting traps and recognizing various species of insects. Those forays usually left me dirty, disheveled, and impatient for the next day's adventures. My appetite, which had always been poor, improved. My face flushed with color, and my hair brightened.

Toward the end of our stay, Father would come to Krynica for a week or two while Mother went back to Katowice. But wonderful as these vacations were, they could not compare with our visits to my grandparents in Dabrowa, a small town of a few thousand inhabitants set in the midst of bucolic villages and stunning conifer forests. Dabrowa was about twenty kilometers from Tarnów, the nearest city.

Mother and Father were born in Dabrowa, and their parents were at that time still living there. Both families owned and lived on their land. That was unusual for Jews, who, history shows, had to be ready at a moment's notice to pack up and leave some countries when a king or a president decided to expel them. Such conditions did not lend themselves to the purchase of land. The Jews in Poland favored investments in smaller, portable things. I wonder today how both sets of my grandparents had the courage to own real estate. I also wonder how long they had owned it: had it been in the family for generations or was it a recent acquisition?

Father's family had wealth in their real estate and stables of horses while Mother's parents referred to themselves as nouveau poor, given their current circumstances. My great-grandparents were dead, so I knew nothing of their background, but from Mother I learned that Grandmother came from a family who owned land and a large house with servants.   Grandmother had married for love against her parents' advice. She had been attracted to Grandfather by his good education and his interpretation of Jewish laws. When they married, Grandfather was a poor yeshiva student (he later became a teacher), and Grandmother brought to her marriage the house they lived in, nothing else.

Father's well-to-do family included merchants as well as horse traders. He was the oldest of three boys, but his three sisters were all older than he. Father's home in Dabrowa was a U-shaped building surrounded by acres of hilly orchards. Removed from the house by a short walk were whitewashed stables with walls covered by a profusion of wildly climbing wisterias.

Behind the house was a group of low, grass-covered, cavernous hills. There was only one entrance to the caverns, which were joined by a series of arches leading from one cave to another; they stretched for hundreds of feet deep into the darkness, floors strewn with broken bricks, stones, and animal bones. I remember these caves mostly from later years when during World War II, I explored them with friends.

I visited my paternal grandparents only once before the war, as a very young child. They both died shortly after that visit, and everyone said that they had died young. I don't know the details. My grandfather was a burly, red-haired man who loved horses and children. His wife was short and stout. I remember them hugging and kissing me a lot and giving me things to eat and to play with. Their portraits, which hung in my parents' bedroom in Katowice, were more real to me than the visit when I met them. Because I knew my maternal grandparents better, I remember and cherish the memories of those visits most. I vividly remember Grandmother's velvety complexion, crossed by a maze of fine lines I was sometimes allowed to stroke; I also remember her high forehead full of ridges, which her daughters and some granddaughters inherited, and her big blue eyes. She wore a blond wig in accordance with Jewish orthodox law, which prescribes the shaving of a woman's head after marriage so she will not be attractive or enticing to men other than her husband.

Grandfather was very tall. His beard the color of clouds reached down his chest, making him look like a prophet. No figure was more imposing than that of my grandfather when on Friday evenings (the beginning of Shabat), in his long, black silk coat and fur-trimmed hat, a crackling white shirt spread across his chest, with his prayer book under his arm, he strode quickly to the synagogue. Years later, while World War II was raging, Father was honored to serve as cantor during holidays, when one was needed, and I felt a different kind of pride. My father, clean shaven, in Western clothes, blond hair closely cropped, sang in his high tenor, strong and clear. At those times, Mother was proud of her Joske.

The synagogue, a rectangular, rose-colored stucco building facing east, stood on a small, sand-covered piazza. The inside of the synagogue was one long room, with the ceiling above the second floor rounded and lined in cedarwood, stained to a warm mahogany. A single enormous chandelier hung from its middle. Two rows of wooden benches divided the room on the ground floor, and at the far end of it was a door leading to where the Ark of the Covenant was kept. On the second floor, open and visible from the first, was the gallery reserved for women, because in a Jewish orthodox synagogue, women do not sit with men.

Both the south and north walls of the building had four Palladian-style windows, which rose from about five feet off the floor to the women's gallery, rounding off where the ceiling curved upward. When on sunny days the light pouring through these gigantic windows met the cedarwood walls, it created a mellow warmth of such magnitude that it can only be described as heavenly.

I was still little when I first heard Grandmother mention the words *beth hamidrash*, which refer to a hall or school where one studied the Bible, the Talmud, and Hebrew literature. This is where Grandfather spent the better part of each day, studying and teaching the Talmud, which is the book containing Jewish civil and religious laws as well as the commentary (explanation) on these laws. These words, which I never heard in my parents' home, held mysterious meanings. I wanted to go with Grandfather, but because I was a girl, I could not. Boys did not study with girls, and girls did not formally study the Talmud. I became fascinated with the idea that God could manage my life, my parents' lives, in fact everyone's life. I wanted to obey His laws so as not to make Him angry, but I only obeyed those laws at Grandmother's. No one in Katowice pressured or reminded me to do so. I began questioning Mother about religion, and she explained those details from the Talmudic laws that Grandfather had taught her. Mother was actually well versed in Jewish law, and from her I learned a great deal about Judaism.

* * *

Grandmother's house was divided into three apartments. My grandparents occupied the two-room apartment on the right side as one entered the building. Grandmother kept it shiny and polished. The two large windows in the front room, facing south, were unadorned, and the light that entered through them flooded that sitting-eating-cooking room. In the back room stood my grandparents' large mahogany bed. I was born in that bed and put at once in swaddling clothes, in which I remained imprisoned for months.

On the opposite side of the house lived an egg merchant with his wife and daughter, and in back lived a widow, Mindy, with her daughter, Dolores. I sometimes visited the widow. She was a gentle soul who rarely left her home, living like a hermit. Her apartment was dark and smelled sweetly of cloves. Because the house was built on an incline and her part of it was lower than the front of the building, two steps led down to her sitting room. Here, by a north window, she worked on wigs that people from the neighborhood brought for styling and repairs. In this heavily populated Jewish orthodox neighborhood, many married women wore wigs, and the widow was kept busy from morning till night. Her daughter, a woman well advanced in years, ran errands and kept house.

I paid more frequent visits to the lively home of the egg merchant. Rachel, the merchant's teenage daughter, liked my visits. The egg merchant was a short, heavy man, with bulging eyes and a black beard. His wife and daughter were also short and heavy. I loved watching them count eggs into dozens or break cracked eggs into a large container out of which they would be sold, by the quart, for baking. The traffic in this house was constant—people came to buy eggs, to discuss local politics, and to gossip. Here I also saw how people bargain for lower prices. All of this took place in the front room, where all the furnishings, wall cabinets, and walls were painted white.

The back room was off limits to everyone, including me—it was this family's sanctuary. I glimpsed it a few times when Rachel and I were alone. The room contained a gigantic bed covered in red silk. There were knickknacks on tables, a dresser with mirror, and a small cot made up with a large pillow and feather bed. I guess that's where Rachel slept. The floor was painted red, and small flowered rugs were placed artistically around the bed and cot. A heavy curtain hung on the single window, which faced the courtyard, and save for the crack of light from the front room when the door was opened, the room always stayed in darkness. I tried more than once to look in from the courtyard, but all I could see was the back of the curtain.

Three wooden steps led to the entrance of Grandmother's building, and someone was always sitting on the top step watching the world go by. So many people sat there for so many years that the top step had a deep groove in it from constant use. It was also my favorite place, especially after dinner, when I wasn't allowed far from home.

One of Mother's friends lived near the railroad station. This meant that from Jagielonska Street, where we stayed with Grandmother, we had to walk across market square and down a beautiful tree-lined avenue of handsome houses. Mother's friend lived in a brown-shingled house surrounded by a garden of flowers. I liked playing in the garden, but the house frightened me because it was dark inside and out, and because the woman's husband was a dentist. I always thought that our visits there had another motive, and that I would have to submit to an examination of my teeth.

But Mother's closest friend in Dabrowa was Rachel, where we visited each spring during our visits to Grandmother. Rachel and Mother had gone to school together and shared secrets of boyfriends from their youth. I loved visiting Rachel; she was warm and affectionate. I also loved her homemade ice cream. Mother corresponded with Rachel during the winter, and when we visited Grandmother, the two friends would catch up on the details.

In good weather groups of people stood around the streets of Dabrowa talking over world affairs. As Mother and I made our daily rounds, people stopped us for a greeting or a chat. Everyone knew Mother. One of my favorite people was Rolla, a deaf mute who also lived on Jagielonska Street. Whenever we were in Dabrowa, Rolla would stand in front of Grandmother's windows to get a look at me. And whenever she saw me leave the house, she followed or stood watch over me while I played, muttering unintelligible words, smiling, and making sure no harm came to me. She became my self-appointed guardian. No one outside my family was allowed to touch me when she was near. I got used to her tall, gaunt frame, her leathery face, and the wiry black and silver hair that framed her face like a tiara—long spikes sticking out all around her head. I expected her near me whenever I left the house. When she was not there, I crossed the street and jumped up and down in front of her windows, hoping she would see me and come out.

If Rolla were living today she would be receiving all the many helpful services to which people with disabilities are now entitled, but because she lived more than fifty years ago, she was the freak of the town. People avoided or made fun of her. It took a small child to understand and appreciate her.

Life in Dabrowa was bountifully decorated with trees, gardens, orchards, birds, insects, butterflies, goats, and cows. These things helped give real meaning to the stories my parents read to me in Katowice. The greenery and sunshine, unobstructed by tall buildings; the friendliness of the people; and the informality were the things I loved about my visits to Grandmother's.

Four

In the spring of 1938, a telegram arrived in Katowice announcing that Grandfather had passed away. Mother left for Dabrowa at once and was gone several weeks. When she returned, she told us that most of the townspeople had turned out for Grandfather's funeral, and his students had carried his casket. Weeks and even months were passing, but Mother continued to mourn, weeping whenever someone offered sympathy.

To me, Grandfather's death was a shock I poorly understood. Uppermost in my mind was that he would not be there when we visited. Some nights I woke crying until Bronia's bed was moved next to mine so that I could be comforted by her.

As I neared my seventh birthday, I was enrolled in a nearby elementary school. On the first day of school, mothers accompanied their children. Wearing white stockings, patent leather shoes, and a navy blue dress with matching cape and hat, I walked the three blocks from my house, holding a foil-covered cardboard cone filled with candy and tied with ribbons. The cone was a custom for first graders, and the candy was to be shared by all. It was so large that it covered the upper part of my body.

All around the school grounds moved photographers who, for a little money, were snapping pictures of parents with their children "on the first day of school." Mother and I had our picture taken, and Mother gave the photographer our address. When he delivered the photograph, she asked to have it enlarged, and that's how I remember that day, a photo of Mother and me in a silver frame on a bureau in my parents' bedroom—Mother towering in a dark coat that reached her ankles, and me, small, shy, half hidden behind the foil-covered cone, smiling.

Also in my parents' bedroom, next to the portraits of Father's parents, hung a large portrait of a crying golden-haired girl with huge green eyes, a ball in her hand. That was Lena, my sister, who died before I was born.

To complete the school curriculum, Mother enrolled me in Hebrew school, where I would attend three classes a week to learn the language of my ancestors. I would also continue gymnastics, which I had been attending from age five, and a weekly piano lesson. All of these activities kept me away from home most of the day. That left Bronia with nothing to do, so she eventually found another position. I was very upset to see her go, and I blamed Mother for not finding something for her to do. Mother assured me that Bronia was ready to give someone else a few happy years just as she had given them to me. I saw Bronia only one more time when she visited on our first school holiday. She brought me a slice of chocolate layer cake with a segment of orange on top.

By the time I entered school, I already knew how to read— Mother had taught me the alphabet, and looking through my storybooks, I joined the letters to get meaning. So when I brought home my first reader, I read it to Mother with enthusiasm. She supervised my homework and insisted on a neat copybook, with the letters well formed and no erasures, because they made the work look sloppy. In those circumstances, it sometimes took hours to complete a first-grade homework assignment.

Walking by myself to and from school, I began to feel for the first time the thrill of independence. In school I met a girl who lived near our building, and we started walking together. My new friend's name was Maryla, and the novelty of having a close friend added a new dimension to my life. Under her tutelage, I began to openly resent being watched over by Mother and being treated or talked to by Father as if I were a baby. I also found Father's permissive kindness embarrassing. I did not want Maryla to know about it.

Maryla and I often met after lunch to do homework. We usually met at my house, and she often copied my work surreptitiously. Her parents were in the wholesale fruit business. Her house was always noisy, full of people. Maryla's mother was fat and loud.

**First Day of School,
with Mother and Cousin Zela**

As a contrast to my own mother, she fascinated me, primarily because she ignored me and didn't seem to pay any attention to Maryla. Sometimes Mother would let me go straight from school to Maryla's for dinner, where we ate heavy bean soups, boiled beef, and the like. Desserts were always fresh fruit, often fruit out of season. It was quite different from what I was used to, and I thought it wonderful. No one stood over me to see if I had finished my food, and I could refuse any course without being reprimanded for it.

As winter passed and days got warmer, Maryla and I often met after lunch in the park. At first a nanny or a family member would come along, but after a while we were allowed to go by ourselves. Still, I often saw Bronia lingering with her new charge some distance away.

On one spring day, a boy in our class asked if I was going to be in the park that afternoon. I said yes, to which he responded, "be there at three." I reddened and on the way home told Maryla about my date. She said she would come with me, and when we met, I was surprised that she had brought two other girls along. The boy, Josef Graf, brought along a number of boys as well, and I was grateful to Maryla for bringing the girls.

Josef and I never actually met on that day. The boys stayed several yards away from us, joking and laughing and calling out "Josef loves you." We, in turn, observed them and talked among ourselves, conjecturing what their next move would be. We waited in vain for something dramatic to happen, but the boys were not very creative, and eventually we all went home. When I saw Josef next morning in class, he hit me in the arm as he passed. I interpreted this to be love.

My friendship with Maryla did not last beyond that first school year. She found a new friend and abruptly broke off our friendship. The disappointment of this loss prevented me from allowing myself to have a close friend again for a long time. The following September, we were assigned to different classes, and Maryla and I did not renew our friendship.

In addition to books I read for school, I began to read more serious books for young people. I remember reading a series of novels by a Russian writer who was very popular at that time. The heroine in those books was called Nina, and after finishing the series, I refused for a time to answer to any name but Nina. Mother and Father learned to call me Nina if they wanted a response. Of course, at school I still responded to Sala. (My birth certificate actually said Sarah, but I was called Sala by friends and family, which I assume is the biblical name translated into Polish.)

History repeats itself. Years later, when my daughter went away to camp for the first time at age nine, I received a card from her signed Flourette. I was momentarily stumped, not knowing who the card was from, but upon examining the handwriting and content, I realized that it was from my daughter and that she probably wished to be called Flourette, having heard or read the name somewhere.

Mother's brother, Herman, and her two sisters, Franka and Gusta, and their spouses all lived in Katowice and kept in close touch. The three sisters saw each other almost daily to gossip and to read each other's mail from friends and family. Aunt Franka, the middle sister, a raven-haired beauty with beguiling blue eyes, was married to my father's brother Emil. They had no children and were very well off. In fact, I remember my uncle as a money giver. "Buy something with this which your mother won't let you have." He would wink as he put silver coins in the palm of my hand.

They lived in a handsome apartment slightly past city limits. Visiting Aunt Franka was a challenge: we had to remove our shoes in the hall to avoid tracking dirt in from the street. Food was served in the kitchen or, in summer, on the terrace to prevent crumbs from falling onto the rugs. We rarely visited there. Instead, Franka visited us every afternoon. My mother had a very close relationship with that sister. Both women's husbands were often away from home, and family closeness kept up their interest in each other, but not because they had things in common—they couldn't have been more different. Perhaps because of her beauty, Aunt Franka was vain and self-centered.

Her husband indulged her every whim. I never perceived any self-centeredness in my mother.

Aunt Gusta, the youngest of the three, lived with her husband and two children, Zela and Moniek, only a few streets away from us, and it would have been easy to drop in there daily, but Aunt Gusta was married to a man the family did not approve of, and that made things awkward. Still, Mother made it a point to call there several times a week, and I was very fond of both my cousins. Their large apartment lent itself to many exciting games, such as hide and seek and other games requiring space. Mona and Bertold, two elderly brothers, rented a small portion of Aunt Gusta's apartment. They were Germans who spoke no Polish. Moniek spent every free minute with these two men, who thoroughly indoctrinated him with a passion for all things German, including the language, which he had spoken fluently for as long as I could remember him.

Zela, a little older than I, considered herself socially above her younger brother and me. When her friends were around, she disdainfully called me her "little cousin." Zela wore matching outfits and carried a pocketbook, where she kept a handkerchief and a tiny purse with change.

Moniek was blond, blue eyed, and wore Tyrolean lederhosen. That alone made him intriguing, let alone his good looks. Too bad for me we were the same age and he hated girls. But despite all the posturing, the three of us looked forward to our visits.

Mother's brother, Herman, was a happy-go-lucky young man who, as the baby in the family, was thoroughly spoiled, doing only what he wanted to do and rarely what was expected of him. He had no profession. His main occupation seemed to have been playing cards and sitting around the many coffeehouses in town. Uncle Herman wore sports clothes during the day and always changed into a dark suit for the evening.

He eventually married a fine lady a few years older than he. Aunt Roosia brought a large dowry to this marriage, and that, as far as Uncle was concerned, was her most important asset, while it took her only a moment after she met him to fall madly in love. Aunt Roosia was not considered pretty, but the sweetness of her character endeared her to everyone who knew her, including me. After the wedding, Uncle gave up his bachelor quarters, and they moved into an apartment in our building. This nearness gave her an opportunity to get to know her husband's sisters, and indeed, she was a welcome addition to their get-togethers. They loved gathering to read letters from friends and family. There was often much laughter when the sisters impersonated various characters they knew in Dabrowa. I was convinced that these shows were put on to entertain Roosia.

Her happiness didn't last very long. Within a few months, Aunt Roosia began complaining about Herman's late nights out. When pressed to spend more time at home, he planned his evenings around card games with friends, which often lasted until morning. Mother tried to settle their disputes, listening to both sides, but he was not interested in Mother's opinions and refused her help in resolving their difficulties,

On days when I was not busy with school, Mother sent me to visit Aunt Roosia, who was always happy to see me. She would open the door, a broad smile on her face, her arms open wide, ready for a hug. She enjoyed combing my hair, and she didn't tire of saying, "it feels like silk," gently tucking every stray strand into the braids.

During those rare times when Uncle was home, he sat and watched his wife braiding my hair, and when she was finished, he would walk over to me, tug at my nose, and say, "It turns up too much. Let's pull it down some." He joked, did card tricks, and asked questions about my schoolwork as Aunt Roosia looked on happily. No doubt she dreamed of having her own child someday, but it was difficult to imagine Uncle Herman domesticated.

In spite of their problems, Herman and Roosia remained together until the war broke out. At that time, they both decided to go back to their respective parents, and Uncle promised to join her as soon as it became clearer what conditions the war would impose on us. He was the first, in 1939, to return to Dabrowa and take up residence with Grandmother.

* * *

The majority of Jews in Dabrowa lived in and around the center of town—a large cobble-stoned square surrounded on all four sides by two-story buildings painted in soft shades of rose and yellow.

Out of the two western corners of the square ran two avenues. One was cobble-stoned and flanked by acacia trees, leading downhill to the railroad station. This was probably the most exclusive neighborhood in the town, and it was down this road that Mother and I would travel to visit her friend whose husband was a dentist. Homes along this avenue were large and well kept, each with its own garden. Very few Jewish families lived there. The other, a dirt-packed road, led to Tarnów, the nearest city. Horse-drawn wagons traveled that road, which was equally well kept, with several government buildings at its entrance and large private homes farther down. Aunt Raisa's home was on that avenue.

On the east side of the square, two unpaved streets, crowded with single-story houses, some attached, led out of town to the surrounding villages. These two streets were populated by Jews.

All around the square many of the buildings housed grocery stores, tailor shops, hardware stores, and cobblers. There was also a fancy wood-paneled apothecary, where an elderly gentleman filled prescriptions. During the war, Mother was a frequent patient there.

An important part of the square was the loggia projecting from the side of a long building. This whitewashed, shaded area was a popular meeting place for everyone from young people to professionals and merchants of all kinds. During the war, I once watched a man selling fruit juice there out of a tin tub. Many people stopped for refreshment, and some did not finish their glass. Standing nearby, I saw the man pour the leftovers back in the tub. I was a mere child, and he paid no attention to me. A swindler, I thought and felt sorry for all the trusting customers who drank his juice.   Once a week, on market day, the square filled with farmers and merchants: big burly farmers calling out loud greetings to friends, their wives setting up stands for the display of eggs, butter, and vegetables; stacks of chicken pens with clucking chickens inside and screaming geese; horses snorting and pawing cobblestones; laughter. Pale Jews in dark suits, their ear locks folded behind their ears, piled up their stands with shirts, socks, shoelaces, and boot polish, their wives standing timidly on the side holding cashboxes. Uncle Meyer was there too, with his best horses, ready to make deals. Throngs of people jostled around.

Grandmother and I would wind our way through this friendly cacophony, I holding on to her while she bargained for a pound of butter or a chicken. What excitement, what a thrill to be a part of this. These experiences did not exist in Katowice, where I did not know where the food served at the table came from.

Dabrowa had no sewers, electricity, or plumbing. Baths were taken in great wooden tubs, and in each house stood a large tin barrel where water was stored for daily use. This water was delivered from the town's four wells in the center of market square. Professional water carriers would fill their cans, which hung on chains or heavy cord from a wooden yoke. Then, swinging the yoke across their shoulders, they would run in all directions of town with small rapid steps, moving their bodies from side to side to keep time with the rhythm provided by the weight of the cans.

About a year before World War II broke out, a letter arrived from Grandmother informing us that electricity had come to Dabrowa and that she would have it brought into her house. Later, when we lived there, light bulbs hung from many ceilings. It was strange to see the brightly lit windows in the evenings. I preferred the comforting glow of the kerosene lamps.

When we visited Dabrowa, Mother and I would go mushroom gathering. Early on a fine August morning, we would start down Jagielonska Street and just keep walking until the sidewalk ended and the town was behind us. Passing fields of ripening corn, rye, and wheat that reached Mother's head, we walked in narrow paths as if in a maze, eventually reaching an open meadow, where many-colored cows grazed under the not-too-watchful eye of a dozing shepherd. Reaching the thick growth of prickly blackberry and raspberry bushes, which so often surrounded the pine woods, we looked for an entrance into the forest. Once inside, we stopped for a moment on the soft, needle-covered ground to get used to the change in light and to inhale the fragrance of pine. It was dark here, still and cool. One fourth of Poland is forests, and none is more beautiful than those around Dabrowa.

Mother taught me to recognize edible mushrooms, and there were many varieties, some more desirable than others. Especially sought after was the edible boletus, with its large brown cap and stout white stem. Mother pointed out that under this mushroom's cap was a porous, foamlike thickness instead of the usual gills found in other mushrooms. The boletus was rare, and I still remember the thrill we felt whenever we spotted one standing in solitary splendor under a pine tree. If one of us saw it, she called the other to look at it before plucking it out of the ground. It was so wonderful to find a boletus that it had to be shared; it had to be savored.

These mushrooms could be dried and saved for winter to use in soups and sauces. Mostly, though, we gathered bright yellow chanterelles, which grew in abundance. They would be sautéed in butter and onion, their delicious fragrance filling the house. When our baskets were full, we would go to the edge of the wood and fill a pot with raspberries. Then, carrying our precious finds, we would start the walk back home.

In Dabrowa we also made the usual rounds of calls on Mother's friends, and wherever we visited, I had to recite poems of which I had a large repertoire committed to memory. Being timid, I needed much coaxing to get started. A particular poem that still stays in memory is Julian Tuwim's lengthy "Lokomotywa" (Locomotive). I performed this with all the sounds and motions of a moving train. At those times, all eyes were centered on me, and Mother sat transfixed, a proud grin on her face. Today, this may seem trivial and naive, but then, it was part of a life of grace and pleasure.

Five

In 1938, the Germans began burning synagogues and breaking windows in Jewish shops in Germany. In 1939, Hitler, as chancellor of Germany, expelled all Jews from that country, and during one of our visits to Aunt Gusta's, we saw, from the living room windows, scores of people coming from various directions, carrying small bundles, apparently looking for shelter. These people were German Jews who, when they were expelled from their country, were not allowed to take more than a change of clothes with them. Most simply took the train to Poland, and many got off in Katowice.

Aunt Gusta eventually took in a man with his teenage son while they looked for a home of their own. They told terrible stories of violence done against them. Both boy and father were in shock. They spoke in whispers.

German Jews never considered themselves anything but Germans, loving their country and being proud to be German. They were so integrated into German society that being suddenly singled out as Jews in order to be expelled was a wholly unexpected jolt.

Similar unrest and open hatred for Jews soon followed in Poland. By September 1939, an ordinance had taken effect, forbidding Jewish and Christian children to attend the same schools. In Katowice Jewish children had to attend a school on the outskirts of town. To get to school on time, I left home before seven in the morning and caught the tram, which I rode for forty-five minutes. On the way I encountered daily discrimination in subtle and not so subtle ways. Conversing among themselves, people looked around at those of us who were going to school and commented, "Look at the little Jews going to school." For the first time, I felt the biting venom of hatred. Protected and shielded from all harm by my parents, I had always felt that Poland was my country—that I belonged.

Now it dawned on me that my home—my country—was not really my home, that I was an unwanted outsider. That feeling of not belonging was the most intense and the most painful I had ever experienced.

Mother explained why I could not attend the school in our neighborhood that I had grown to love. And with what I heard on the tram and what I occasionally experienced when taking walks with friends, I realized that being Jewish was not a good thing to be, that it was, in fact, dangerous. I felt acutely the impediment of belonging to a distinct group instead of to the world at large. I felt inferior—inferior because I was losing my sense of security. Realizing that who I was was not a good thing to be left me reeling with a worry akin to that of skating on thin ice that at any moment might crack.

From those non-Jews Father knew in high places, he learned that very soon the kind of life Jews had enjoyed in Poland until 1939 would change radically. Mother knew, too, from speeches by Jabotinsky, a charismatic orator who inspired many young people to emigrate to Palestine with a view to restoring that country to the Jews, and from other sources that there was much to fear in the near future. However, I am convinced that neither of my parents even vaguely imagined the horrors that lay in store for us, because had he known, Father would have prepared some escape.

Up to that time, whenever the question of emigration had come up, Father had always shrugged it off by saying that people who are successful where they live do not emigrate. He had no plans to leave Poland. It wasn't until he heard the predictions for the future that he contacted his oldest sister, Dora, in Fayetteville, North

Carolina, about helping us (as well as Aunt Franka and Uncle Emil) emigrate to America.

Aunt Dora wasted no time starting the paperwork on her end, and Father went to the American consulate in Warsaw to start the process from our end. This was when an Englishman was engaged to teach us the English language, when we met twice each week around the dining room table to learn. Being occupied with his business, Father often missed these lessons, and Uncle Emil never attended. Uncle Herman, Mother, Aunt Franka, and I made good progress and often remained together after the lesson to converse in English.

None of us was especially eager to leave our comfortable life in Poland for an unknown country. With the exception of a few inconveniences, such as spending a lot of time on the tramway going to school, being called a scabby Jewess, or having an occasional rock thrown at me, life continued to be good. I tried to forget these insults, not to make them linger, and at times I was successful. Soon these insults became a part of life—an upsetting part to be sure, but because I grew to expect them, they were not as painful as they had been when I was first surprised by them.

At home nothing changed. All comforts were still there: Father, forever loving; Mother, watchful and guiding, always home, ready to comfort; the household help; the food; my lovely white bed. At school I excelled in language and (with Mother's help) in drawing, and I was placed in first bench with two slow students to assist them. I never volunteered for extra activities; I was too shy. But by the end of my third year, when our class put on a play, I accepted a small dancing part to the music of *Coppélia* by Léo Delibes. Mother and Aunt Franka came to watch.

As the school year drew to a close, Mother made plans to send me away for the summer. I would be away from my parents for the first time. With the help of Doctor Sachs, who suggested that at age eight I should be on my own for a while, I was sent to a camp in the Carpathian Mountains in Poland. A hired car and driver picked up Mother and me and our suitcases, and we drove off to join the many other children going to camp in Rabka.

When we arrived at our destination, Mother went through the formalities of checking me in and going with me to a room with two rows of bunk beds, where she emptied my suitcase and arranged the clothes in my locker. Then, with a kiss on my forehead, she left.

I sat down on my bed and cried. A few minutes later, a girl came in, sat down next to me, and we both cried. But as the room began to fill up, we forgot about crying and started looking around, observing other girls being settled in—some by their parents, some alone.

That evening a counselor took us to an immense room with showers, and for the first time, I took a shower. At home I had always taken baths. Afterward we were shown how to fold our clothing, and we got into our bunks. Mine was a lower bunk, and never having seen a bed like it, I thought it quite possible that the upper bunk would fall on me. Lights went out while it was still daylight. Lying on the hard mattress, afraid the upper bunk would fall, I felt like an orphan. This only triggered familiar thoughts and fears of losing my parents—prophetic thoughts. That fear would sometimes be so obsessive that I would need to be close to Mother, entreating her not to die. Yet here I was, abandoned (I felt) by all those whom I trusted and who loved me.

In the morning, I thought, I'm going to call home and have Mother pick me up—I am not going to stay in this place. Looking up at the slats of the upper bunk, I thought, What is Bronia doing now? Is Mother staying in Rabka overnight, and if so, is the driver staying here also so he can drive her home tomorrow? Where is Father? Following no particular order, these random thoughts occupied me until a piercing bell rang in the hall, and immediately afterward, the noise of many voices and footsteps brought me back to where I was. Yes, I was in camp, and it was morning, the next day.

A counselor rushed into the room, calling out a cheerful good morning and giving a smart slap across somebody's rear end. "Up, everybody, up, girls, it's a beautiful morning, and we have a lot to do. Get dressed and go to the washroom to wash your face, hands, and brush your teeth." With that, she assisted those of us who could not manage on our own. I needed help with braiding my hair. With much calling out, instructing, and running back and forth, all in a cheerful, helpful manner, the girls got ready. Those who had been in camp before helped those who had not.

We lined up in pairs in front of the door and, following the counselor's lead, walked out into a field of grass, surrounded by lush green mountains, the sky above pale pink, fair-weather clouds drifting across it. The sun was barely visible on the horizon. It was wonderful to be alive, the world was beautiful, and everything was right.

Already waiting for us—we were apparently the youngest group—were children of varying ages standing around a large square. When everyone was in his proper place and totally silent, a male voice started the first line of the beautiful Polish prayerlike song "Kiedy Ranne Wstają Zorze" (When Morning Dawn Rises) and was soon joined by a chorus of voices trained and rehearsed to follow. The song rose to the sky in exquisite harmony. I was impressed with its powerful magnificence, and I resolved to learn this song so that I could sing along each morning. To this day, when I take an early morning walk and watch the sun rise, my lips automatically form the first lines of "Kiedy Ranne Wstają Zorze."

Breakfast, however, was a different matter. Watery hot chocolate, scrambled eggs—my least favorite food—and worst of all, we were allowed only fifteen minutes to eat. I could not even get through a third of my food in that amount of time. But when leaving the table with most of my breakfast still untouched, I was relieved that no one said anything.

With each passing day, I thought less and less about home. I didn't feel lonely, and I hadn't had any attacks of fear. I enjoyed the outdoor activities on good-weather days and the indoor activities on rainy days. I learned knitting, crochet, and a simple form of origami. I learned also to recognize and name various trees and other plants during long, arduous walks. I learned how good it felt to get hungry because no one coaxed me to eat—I ate only what I wanted. I made friends, and we promised to write to each other "forever."

Then came the day when Mother was to pick me up, and even though camp now seemed like home, I was excited about returning to Katowice. When I entered my room at home, the old familiar fear came over me again, but this time it did not last; there were too many exciting things to talk about. Mother was my curious listener, supplying a flow of questions and compliments.

When the excitement of camp died down, I observed a change in our domestic atmosphere. My parents were nervous; their talks lasted late into the night, and the topic was politics or our emigration to America. Father went once more to Warsaw to see if our paperwork could be speeded up so that we might leave sooner because war seemed imminent, but at the American consulate, he was informed that nothing could be done for us specifically and that our papers were being processed on schedule. He was told that countless names crowded waiting lists of people who had applied for visas years before us, all of whom now clamored to emigrate. Even if it were possible to secure space for crossing over, others came before us. Father returned home depressed because he could not take us to a safe place.

Instead, plans were quickly made for Mother and me to go to Grandmother's in Dabrowa, that sleepy little town where the twentieth century had not yet arrived. No one at that time even remotely imagined that the Germans would have any interest in Dabrowa, where plumbing was still unknown and electricity had only recently come to town. It seemed a safe place to be.

Trunks and suitcases were packed and sent ahead. Father would remain in Katowice to liquidate his business. A maid would stay to keep house until he was ready to leave. Aunts Gusta and Franka and my two cousins Moniek and Zela would also leave for Dabrowa, but they would wait a while longer, hoping that the rumors of war would prove to be untrue. Both Gusta's and Franka's husbands remained in Katowice to close their businesses.

When in August of that year Russia, who was supposed to be one of the Allies, signed a nonaggression pact with Germany, we knew we were at a precipice. The year was 1939.

Dabrowa

Six

For as long as I could remember, I had wanted to live in a tiny farmhouse such as I had seen in the villages around Dabrowa. These cottages consisted of one large room with a tightly packed dirt floor, a big stove for cooking, and a side compartment for baking built into a concrete wall. In the room were about three or four benches that, when their seats were lifted, revealed straw-filled sackcloth mattresses that served as beds. The rest of the furnishings usually consisted of a large wooden table, chairs, an urn used for bringing in milk from the barn for family use, a barrel with water for cooking and drinking, and a kerosene lamp. A crucifix and perhaps one or two holy pictures decorated the whitewashed walls.

Most of these cottages were kept immaculately clean. They were painted white outside as well as in and were surrounded by vegetable and flower gardens. Their utter simplicity and coziness appealed to me. Arriving in Dabrowa for an indefinite period, I hoped my long-dreamed-of fantasy of living in one of those houses would come true. And in a way, it did, but much later, and it was hardly as romantic as I had imagined it would be.

Our arrival in Dabrowa created a lot of excitement, as usual. It gave people something to talk about. Everyone knew us. Grandmother sent a fiacre to the station to pick us up—she rarely ventured far from home—and as we rode into town, many people waved hello. I was happy to be back in Dabrowa. It felt like a holiday trip.

As we got off at Grandmother's house, a group of people, mostly children, gathered around to watch. Happy to see us,

Grandmother had food and drink all ready, and while Mother and I sat at the table, she stood over me smiling, stroking my hair, and urging me to eat and not to play with my food. At the same time, she plied me with questions—"What grade are you in now? Tell me about what you are studying"—which I answered to her satisfaction. She praised the good language I used and nodded her head approvingly in Mother's direction. I was more interested in going out to talk to the children in the street, or at least to look at them. Some were sitting on the sidewalk playing with marbles, and some just stood around waiting for me to come out. Their clothes were dirty, and they didn't wear shoes. There were many barriers between us, not the least of which was language—I didn't speak Yiddish, and they didn't speak Polish. But I enjoyed just sitting on Grandmother's front stoop and communicating with smiles. They stared, touched my clothes, and said things I did not understand.

Despite the grinding poverty suffered by most Jews in Dabrowa, somehow everyone had a roof over their heads and food on the table. Everyone managed, and those who couldn't were helped by those who were able.

Some, like the grain merchant, Mr. S., in his beautiful three-story house, the doctor, the dentist, and the druggist with his elegant apothecary, lived on the outskirts of town, educating their children abroad. But the majority of Jews in Dabrowa belonged to the tightly knit community of craftspeople and traders, accepting their subsistence good naturedly from generation to generation.

Save for Mr. S.'s house at the end of Jagielonska Street, just where the town ended, Grandmother's was one of the prettiest and best-kept houses on that street. It was always meticulously whitewashed, the double wooden entrance stained brown, windows shining. I could not invite anyone to play inside because Grandmother would not tolerate disorder in her home. In no time, however, the grain merchant and his wife, who had four grown sons and an eighteen-year-old daughter, Eva, married to a man twenty years her senior, gave me free reign of the first floor in their home. That floor was used as a granary, where wheat, rye, and barley were stored. The entire floor of beautiful, high-ceilinged rooms was filled with cool grain in which I romped around and buried myself up to my neck to stay cool on warm summer days.   The S. family occupied the two upper stories of this cream-colored sandstone mansion. Eva, with her husband and infant daughter, Gigi, lived in a small one-story house attached to the main residence. The two middle sons worked in a government office in Dabrowa, and the oldest son, who had recently returned from abroad with a medical degree, was busy setting up office.

Sometimes the youngest of the boys asked me to come to the upper floors, where we might sit on a balcony and talk. And sometimes Mrs. S. called me up for a chat and cookies. I still remember her chestnut hair, always perfectly combed. "What grade are you in school?" she invariably started our conversations. "Third," I would answer, and then I would have to tell her in great detail "what they are teaching" me. Almost the same precise words my grandmother used.

In back of this house was a fenced-in orchard, where gooseberries and currants grew in well-tended rows, and trees bent under their heavy crops of dark red cherries and purple plums. A little round arbor stood on the right as one entered the garden, and I spent many wonderful hours in that arbor, weaving dreams while eating fruit I had just picked. I spent so much time there alone that I got to know each mark in the latticework, in the benches, and in the large table that nearly filled the arbor. I dreamed there of far-off places and of a little peasant hut with a barn filled with fragrant hay and a stall full of cows and horses. Sometimes I imagined Italy,

Mother's dream country. Surrounded in arboreal splendor, often accompanied by music drifting out of Eva's home as she played the piano, I had found the ideal place to dream.

Within a few days of our arrival in Dabrowa, Aunt Gusta arrived with her children, and Aunt Franka was expected any day. Uncle Herman was already installed at Grandmother's.

There were too many of us under one roof, and Aunt Gusta moved in with her in-laws some streets away, taking Zela and Moniek with her. I now had playmates because Zela could not quickly find a suitable friend her own age. She chose to disregard our age difference and called on me daily. Moniek too found it harder to ignore me in these surroundings, where he did not know anyone. And because I had access to the S. family's house and garden, I became a sought-after companion to both my cousins. We played in the rooms filled with grain, inventing games and learning fascinating facts about the different varieties from the men who worked there.

We made no new friends because we all thought we would not remain in Dabrowa for very long. We thought this to be a temporary situation and planned to return to Katowice soon. Our mothers, to all outward appearances, pretended that our lives had not in any way been disrupted, that this was merely a pause before we could resume our old lives in Katowice.

One Saturday afternoon, the three sisters and their mother occupied the two front windows in Grandmother's sitting room, watching passersby, waving to some and commenting among themselves. I was stretched out on the large bed in the next room, reading. The door was wide open between the rooms when I heard Grandmother declare, "There she is, that Eva. Look at the way she struts, looking straight ahead as if she had a purpose—high heels, swinging hips. And she smokes, too. A sure mark of a dissolute woman."

My eyes left the print and glanced toward the windows in the next room. Mother, at that same moment, exchanged silent looks with her two sisters. Aunt Gusta's hand moved from the windowsill to the pocket of her cardigan, slowly pushing down the package of cigarettes she kept there. Grandmother continued, "No wonder she smokes, marrying that old man."

"He is only thirty-eight," said Mother.

"But she is only eighteen," retorted Grandmother sharply.

"He is handsome and rich and a good catch for a girl who is not pretty," said Aunt Franka.

"She may not be pretty, but she knows how to use what she has," joined in Aunt Gusta. "And after all, she is rich, too."

"She certainly knows how to use what she has," said Grandmother. "I saw your brother talking with her for quite a long time. They were laughing as if they shared some private joke!" Grandmother had obviously been bothered by what she had seen. The sisters looked at each other without saying another word.

Of course, it is difficult, if not impossible, to recall with any accuracy a conversation that took place more than fifty years ago, but the gist of this scene has been coming back to me as clearly as if it had happened yesterday. It was memorable because I was a child when it happened, and at the time, I felt I had heard something that under different circumstances would not have been said in my presence. And it became even more memorable because of what eventually followed in connection with what I heard on that day. Meanwhile, I remained on the bed, trying to be inconspicuous. I caught sight of Eva when she was returning from town, and I even remember the dress she wore: white silk with red dots, a red belt at her waist.

* * *

By entering Poland on September 1, 1939, Germany started World War II and, meeting virtually no resistance from the Ill-equipped Polish army, invaded two-thirds of the country in a little more than two weeks. The other third of Poland—the eastern part—was invaded by Russia. It took only one month for Poland to cease to exist.

* * *

On a Friday night we all had dinner with Grandmother, and afterward we were sitting in front of the house when suddenly a panic arose in the streets. Within a few minutes, the town was deserted. Taking our chairs inside, we locked the house and went to the windows. Moniek was first to recognize the roar of an engine and declared it to be a motorcycle. Mother recognized the man in dark blue uniform, speeding down our street and stirring up a cloud of dust, as a German policeman. An unbelievable event. Up to that moment, my family did not believe the Germans would bother with a little unimportant town like Dabrowa. No one could have envisioned this town being precisely what the Germans looked for because of its high concentration of religious Jews in one area, ideal for the "final solution" the Germans were planning (the complete eradication of all Jews).

It was still daylight, and some of us went out on the street again to look toward the market, where we could make out the movement of soldiers and their vehicles. That night we all stayed at Grandmother's, sleeping two and three to a bed.

The next morning some people ventured out to the market, and Mother and I were among them. The place was teeming with green-uniformed soldiers and their parked vehicles. We made our way to where a group of officers was talking at the other end of the square. Greeting them in fluent German, Mother asked if Katowice had already been occupied and if it was safe to go back there. Detaching himself from the rest, one officer took out a map and, pointing to it with a pistol, spotted Katowice. He thought for an instant and answered that it was all right to go back; the city was already in German hands. He asked if that was where we were from, commenting on what a lovely city it was and how well Mother spoke German. He said something else in an undertone, and Mother seemed embarrassed. She quickly thanked him for the information, and we left.

Meanwhile, some of the noise around us subsided as dozens of eyes from every corner of the market were on us. People stood around staring, but no one else talked with the Germans. As we walked back home, people asked if it was all right to talk to them, and Mother said yes. Slowly, the paralysis that had gripped the town the night before dissipated.

When Mother told everyone at home that Katowice was "safe," we all became very excited, making plans to return as soon as we heard from Father. Aunt Gusta went back to her in-laws, taking Moniek and Zela along, with Moniek carrying on about how he knew one could trust the Germans and what a fine people they were and how when he grew up, he wanted to be a German.

By the afternoon, the square was clear of soldiers. They had requisitioned the magistrate's building and the public school building and settled some of their men in both places. Parts of Father's ancestral home were also requisitioned, and one of Father's two sisters (one natural and one adopted) who still lived there left for unknown parts of the country. No one heard from her again. The other, Haika, the youngest of the three natural sisters, managed to hold on to two rooms and remained with her husband and infant son until two years later, when the three of them were sent to a concentration camp.

Uncle Meyer, the youngest of Father's brothers, brought his family from Krynica when the summer season ended, and they moved back into their small white house with the large stable nearby. Before the war, I had hardly known that uncle. He left the hotel business in Krynica to his wife while he stayed mostly in Dabrowa. But during the war, I got to know him and his family well. He continued to be absent from home a lot, forever scouring the countryside for young horses, which he brought back to town and sold.

Uncle Meyer was very tall, with dark hair and a swarthy complexion. He laughed easily. In fact, telling jokes and stories, recalling his travels, is how I remember him best. He could keep a room full of people in stitches for hours—it didn't matter if everything he said was true; it sounded wonderful and funny, and that's what mattered. I vividly remember his "Mrs. Korona" story.

After exploring the villages for available horses, he was stranded with his herd in the rapidly falling light of the evening. Uncle decided to seek shelter with an elderly lady, where he occasionally took a meal when in the neighborhood. Mrs. Korona offered a way station for the horses, but she did not take in overnight guests. She had only one large double bed and no other overnight accommodations. Knowing that he would most likely not find a bed anywhere at this time of evening, Uncle begged Mrs. Korona: "I'll sleep in the barn, on the kitchen bench, with my herd in the grass, anywhere," but Mrs. Korona would have none of it and suggested that he sleep on the other half of her bed.

Having fed and watered the horses, Uncle simply took off his riding boots and threw himself on his half of the bed. Within a few minutes, there arose a problem—Mrs. Korona was a noisy snorer. What to do? Uncle's fertile mind worked on a plan. He picked up one of his boots and yelled into it: "Mrs. Korona, please open the door. I need a glass of water." She woke up and went to the door but found no one there. Grumbling but without making any noise because she didn't want to wake Meyer, she lay down and almost at once started snoring again. Uncle repeated his yelling into the boot once more, and she woke again—very angry. When she came back to bed, she said to him, "I will sleep on the porch in the hammock; otherwise, neither of us will get any sleep." And that's how Uncle Meyer got a few hours of sleep that night.

Uncle's wife was quiet and pretty. I saw her always combing her black curly hair but never saying much. Ceska, their daughter, took after her mother, but whereas I did not know my aunt—how could I when she didn't talk?—I got to know Ceska very well during the war and liked her for her sincerity and her intelligence.

Many years after the war, I continued to look for Ceska, just as I looked for other members of my family, hoping that someone had survived, but I could find nothing until the Holocaust survivors became better organized and information of this kind began appearing on computers.

Seven

The Germans left an occupying force in Dabrowa, while the rest marched deeper into Poland.

Weeks passed, and Mother tried to get in touch with Father, who was still in Katowice, but that was a difficult task. Telephone lines were not working, and neither was the post office. Then a telegram arrived from Father, warning us not to plan a return to Katowice—he would somehow write or try to get in touch with us another way soon. When we heard from him again, at greater length, he explained that he had been informed by reliable sources that Katowice was to be made Judenfrei (free of Jews), a new expression that in time we would learn to use daily as town after town in Poland became Judenfrei.

Resigned now to remain in Dabrowa, Mother began asking around for an apartment or a house. It was understood that Aunt Franka and her husband Emil, my Father's brother, would live with Grandmother. She was the only daughter who got along well with Grandmother. It was also clear that Uncle Herman would live with them because he had no other place to go.

The second oldest of Father's sisters, Aunt Raisa, with whom we were friendly from our visits to her hotel in Krynica, owned a beautiful house on the broad avenue that led to Tarnów, and she cheerfully offered us her fully furnished home. That house, although it had a few Jewish neighbors, was mostly surrounded by Christians and by some government buildings, one of which was the magistrate's building, where the Germans were headquartered. We accepted instantly, full of gratitude for her generous offer.

Aunt Raisa, her husband, and her two grown children—a son, Tovek, and a daughter, Yetta—decided to go to the Russian part of occupied Poland, hoping eventually to continue deeper into Russia. Somehow the Russians did not evoke the same kind of dread the Germans did.

It was difficult to cross over to the Russian side, and many people lost their lives trying. But with sufficient money, one could bribe one's way across. Aunt Raisa and family not only crossed over to the Russian side, they walked that vast country and on to Palestine. Along the way, Raisa lost her husband to frostbite and heart failure.

I saw my aunt and two cousins again in 1969 when I visited Israel. My cousins were married and had their own grown children. Aunt Raisa, past eighty, was still alert. She died at eighty-three in her sleep, at home, surrounded by her children and grandchildren.

When she made her offer, Aunt Raisa called on Mother and simply handed her a set of keys to her home, leaving everything intact. They took only the barest essentials with them.

Strangely, now that there seemed ample reason for fear, the attacks I had suffered as a younger child had subsided. Had they been premonitions of disaster? Now that life was daily taking turns for the worse, perhaps I no longer needed to fear phantoms. I never again felt the same despondency that used to beset me. From the earliest moments of the war, I began to develop a strong sense of self-preservation, and that sense grew as the need for it grew.

With a lovely home at our disposal, Mother asked Aunt Gusta to move in with us. So began a few happy weeks. We all got along well in this comfortable home of two bedrooms, a dining and living room, and a big kitchen. We had a radio and even a guitar, which I started strumming, and after a while, I was able to accompany myself when I sang. I also appropriated for myself two very large dolls we found sitting on some of the beds. Both dolls were dressed in satin: a gypsy man in brown pants neatly tucked into patent leather boots and a bright yellow satin shirt tied with a red sash at the waist, and a ballerina in a white tulle tutu with satin bodice and pink satin stockings in toe shoes.

Because there was little else to do, my cousins and I put on plays for our mothers using the dolls as characters, each of us speaking their parts from behind a makeshift stage. At other times, we recited poems, and Moniek wrote and performed angry skits about soldiers of two opposing armies engaged in war. He always performed in German, and in his skits, the Germans always won.

We knew that he had acquired a love for Germany through his association with Mona and Bertold in Katowice, but no one imagined him to be so imbued with passion for the German army. What was it about the Germans that so appealed to him? Was it the uniforms, or the power they exercised with such abandon? Moniek wanted to wear only his lederhosen, which were popular with German youth at that time, even though they were getting short and a little tight as he was outgrowing them. New ones were nowhere available. He also refused to speak any language but German, even when he was not performing. When addressed in Polish, he answered in German.

When electricity had come to Dabrowa a few years before the war, those people who could afford it bought radios. This turned out to be entertainment for most of the town, because people who did not own a radio listened to programs in their neighbors' homes. A few weeks after the German occupation, anti-Jewish edicts, decrees, and proclamations followed one another furiously. One such ordinance ordered all Jews to surrender their radios. They were to be brought to the magistrate's building.

In Aunt Raisa's home, we found a shortwave radio, but we did not surrender it, so it had to be hidden and listened to only late at night. Our mothers listened to news from other countries broadcast in German, and we sometimes even got broadcasts in English. Certain neighbors were invited for midnight broadcasts, and Uncle Herman was a steady visitor for these get-togethers, gluing his ear to the box as the sound faded in and out, a faint green light emanating from the dial, the rest of the house sunk in darkness. These clandestine newscasts were our only source of news. We lived in a vacuum except for bits and pieces brought by those people who were drafted by the Germans for minor clerical and cleaning work. But the news they brought was so fantastic that no one wanted to believe it: for instance, that the Germans had taken most of Poland. That they had all of Czechoslovakia we already knew, but that they were conquering France on another front or that they were bombing England, we did not believe. Most people thought this was propaganda to frighten us, but of course, it was all true, and our nocturnal broadcasts confirmed what we had heard in town.

Moniek was furious that we were disobeying the order to surrender our radio. On several occasions, he screamed as loudly as he could in German, "I will denounce you to the German army. I will tell them that you are all spies!" Petrified, Aunt Gusta tried to reason with him while the rest of us watched dumbstruck, afraid that some unfriendly neighbor or passerby would hear him and that if Moniek did not go to the Germans, those who heard him might. But the radio remained, and the late night news sessions continued.

From Katowice more regular news began to reach us. Father insisted we remain in Dabrowa, although Mother and Aunt Gusta were anxious to return to Katowice, especially because Aunt Gusta's husband, who was also liquidating his business, was more encouraging in his communication. But for the moment our lives took on a steady routine; mornings, both mothers marketed near Grandmother's house, where farmers' wives brought in their produce from the country and usually sold it along the way before reaching market square. Zela, Moniek, and I stayed home during that time, waiting for the water carrier.

On one of those mornings, when both mothers were out, there suddenly erupted a loud commotion and a banging on the front door. When we opened it, three Germans, accompanied by two Polish policemen, pushed us aside as they entered the house. They asked for Mother and, when told she wasn't home, told us to pick out whatever we wanted most and get out of the house. The Polish policemen standing by watched stone faced.

At first we could not understand what they wanted, so we smiled, and Moniek began a conversation. He often went to their headquarters, where he hoped to make friends with the Germans. They let him visit and sometimes even conversed with him; they were probably curious where he came from and surprised that this blond, blue-eyed boy, fluent in German, was Jewish. Their talks with him were mostly monologues on his side. He told them where he lived and where he came from. Seeing his "friends" now in our home, Moniek felt confident, in his utter innocence, that nothing bad could possibly happen to him. But one of the Germans impatiently raised his voice as he ordered, "Do as you are told," ignoring Moniek completely. This still did not dissuade my little cousin. "But we live here. This house was given to us by a relative who is away now. We are supposed to take care of it until they return." He whined, and finally his voice fell to a whisper. No one but Zela and I looked at him. Then the two Polish policemen pushed the three of us into the bedroom and told us in Polish not to procrastinate but to get out as quickly as we could. Shaken out of my stupor while watching Moniek beg, I picked up the gypsy and ballerina dolls quickly and, running back to the entrance of the house, stood in front of the five men, waiting for my cousins, who followed holding some clothing in their hands. For an instant there was silence as we looked up at our five tormentors—three in green uniforms, two in dark blue. Then, one of the Germans, his face contorted by anger, bellowed out, "Now get out of the house and remember never to return here; this house belongs to the Third Reich." Silent tears streaming down his face, Moniek kept turning his head to stare at the Germans as we walked down the front steps and out on the street.

We ran through the streets, crying hysterically. People looked at us and tried asking what had happened, but we kept running until we reached Grandmother's house, where we met our mothers. Between sobs, we told them what had happened, and all five of us cried while Grandmother tried to console us. Mother ran out of the house to go home, not believing what she had just heard. We stopped her with the warning the Germans had given us: "This house belongs to the Third Reich."

We were now left with nothing, and we were homeless. Later that day, when they had calmed down and gotten used to our situation, Mother and Aunt Gusta went back to what had been our home, hoping to get some clothing and needed household items. When they got there, the Germans had already found the radio and were threatening to arrest both of them, but they denied having had any knowledge of it, saying that the house was only on loan and that they had not looked in every corner. The Germans hardly let them talk; they shouted questions without even allowing them to answer: "Who let this house to you? Where are these people? They must be arrested," and on and on. Finally, after some explanation that the owners were in Russia, Mother and Aunt were grudgingly allowed to remove our clothing, some suitcases, and most of the kitchen utensils.

Before that day ended, the whole town knew what had happened, but the incident was mostly discussed behind closed doors. A pall had fallen over the town as the realization of what might happen to each and every one at the hands of the Germans became clear. This was the first serious lesson of the oppressive domination that would follow. Fear would now be a daily companion, uncertainty of who would be the next victim.

We faced immediate practical problems. Where to sleep? There were not enough beds for all of us at Grandmother's, so Zela and I were sent to a certain lady's house for the night. This woman was unmarried, and her mother, with whom she had lived, had recently died. She lived in a fine two-bedroom apartment, which looked immaculate. We were ushered into a shiny room with two big mahogany beds covered with crisp white linen. As soon as the door of the room was closed, we jumped on the beds, thrilled with our good fortune. Taking off one piece of clothing at a time, we laughed and joked about how lucky we were to have this lovely room all to ourselves. When we blew out the kerosene lamp, we talked in the darkness until sleep got the better of us. But a short time later, we both woke in a panic, scratching and picking bugs off our bodies. "What is this?" I called out, and Zela, smothering her hysteria, ran out of bed and struck a match to light up the room. We were horrified. The white sheets were covered with brown bedbugs, and some of them were sticking to our bodies. Ripping off our nightclothes, we each began picking bugs off the other's body. Then, shaking out our day clothes to make sure no bugs were in them, we got dressed and, leaving the kerosene lamp burning, sat on a marble-topped dresser, watching the bedbugs disappear into the crevices of the handsome, polished mahogany bed frames. By the time dawn started creeping in through the windows, there was not a single bug to be seen anywhere. We let ourselves out of the house and ran to Grandmother's as fast as our feet would carry us. That was the second time in the past twenty-four hours that we had run through the streets looking for a safe haven.

The next few days were crowded, to say the least. Aunt Gusta went back to her in-laws, taking Moniek and Zela with her. Mother and I stayed at Grandmother's with Aunt Franka and Uncle Herman. All females slept in Grandmother's large bed, and Uncle Herman slept on a chaise lounge at the foot of the beds.

Everyone was testy. We were crowded, but we remained polite and mindful of each other's privacy. Mother wasted no time asking around for a vacant apartment. We could not remain at Grandmother's, and the lack of space was not the whole reason. More important, Grandmother ordered her daughters around—all of them—as if they were small children, just as Mother sought to impose her authority on her two younger sisters. Having inherited a good deal of Grandmother's controlling nature, Mother could not tolerate being ordered around. Not that Grandmother invited us to stay. She understood the reasons we could not. In addition, she needed to be more independent than having to worry about so many of us. A house full of people brought on nervous attacks that made everyone miserable.

Grandmother would scream out orders to each of us that were to be obeyed at once. She would then sit down very quietly, observing us while we scurried around doing the tasks she'd assigned. When we were finished, Grandmother would tell us to leave the house and stay away until dinner.

These outbursts were not meant only for us children; they included our mothers, Aunt Franka, and any of the men who were at home at that moment. But by dinnertime, all was forgotten and forgiven, and we ate discussing the happenings of the day.

Aunt Gusta, the most independent of the three sisters, never even entertained the thought of moving in with Grandmother.

Grandmother really only got along with Aunt Franka, and she was glad to have that middle daughter live with her, especially because Franka had no children. When Uncle Emil eventually arrived from Katowice, the three of them and Uncle Herman lived harmoniously until 1942, when that household was brutally torn asunder and ceased to exist forever.

Directly across the street from Grandmother's lived a lady in a funny little house, with three dilapidated steps in front of it. The house was slightly askew, leaning toward the house on its right and away from the one on the left. Mother had long ago named it "The Little Witch's House" because it was tiny, leaned to one side, and seemed generally mysterious. It was full of nooks and crannies, and the lady who lived in it was old and bent. But she was far from being a witch. She was, in fact, a warm and generous woman who baked wonderful cakes and cookies for sale, flooding the street with the most irresistible aromas. Her specialty was a large dark molasses cookie.

From my earliest childhood, whenever we visited Grandmother, I crossed the street to buy cookies from this lady. The ritual of buying a cookie was part of the fun. Her kitchen, into which one entered from the outside, was nearly taken up completely with a huge stove built into the wall. On the side of it was an iron door, which opened to reveal a large baking compartment. The room always smelled of fresh baked goods, many of which were special orders waiting to be picked up. I could never buy a cookie without first answering myriad questions the lady put to me.

"Do you know how to bake?"

"No, but my mother is a very good baker. She knows how to make cheesecake that everybody loves and very good poppyseed cake," I responded enthusiastically.

"I see that your Mother is an excellent baker, because these cakes are difficult to bake." The lady was enjoying our conversation, as was I.

Then came a brief tasting session.

"Oh look, this cookie is partially broken. Have it and also the one with the red jam. It's very good," she encouraged.

Finally, I would put down my five groszy and choose a favorite cookie.

In some ways, this house reminded me of the peasant houses that so appealed to me—its quaintness, the whitewashed kitchen, its coziness, and the good smells that always emanated from it. This two-room house became available when the lady decided to move to Tarnów to live with her son, and Mother rented it. She did this for several reasons: it was near the rest of the family; it was located in the Jewish quarter, where we would not be exposed to the virulent anti-Semitism that by then was rampant even in this small town; and it was centrally located to all necessities, such as water, food sources, stores of all varieties, and friends.

Once we moved in, I realized that this was not the hut of my dreams. There were no open spaces outside the house. It was wedged between other houses with barely an inch to spare on either side. There was no barn, no field, and no animals. The kitchen, which had always seemed so intriguing and cozy, was just like any other kitchen now that the stove was not fired and there was no delicious aroma coming from it. But soon Mother gave it her own brand of coziness. It had a wood storage area on one side, where split logs of birchwood stacked up to the ceiling served as natural decoration, and a large window facing the street, with a frilly curtain embellishing its simple wooden frame. The kitchen came with a comfortable table and chairs, and the wide oak floorboards were soon bleached to a near white from scrubbing.

Tiny French doors led to the sitting and sleeping room. At the left of that room was a black iron pot-belly stove for heating, and at the other end was a window out on a tiny courtyard—the only source of light in that room. This room came furnished with such necessities as beds, a table and chairs, a rug, a large wardrobe, and a mahogany-framed mirror, which hung suspended from the wooden molding near the ceiling. There was enough room under the hanging mirror to place our large black trunk, which Mother had filled with clothing and linen in Katowice before shipping it to Grandmother's to await our arrival. Luckily, we still owned that. Mother polished the trunk and put a white embroidered scarf on it, and it became an additional piece of useful furniture.

There was no sidewalk on our side of the street, but cobblestones placed randomly rose up to the first of three wooden steps that led to the entrance of our new home. Looking out the kitchen window, we could see Grandmother's house and everyone who walked on the wide concrete sidewalk on that side of the street. Mother eventually came to spend her afternoon hours sitting at the kitchen window, and people with whom she was friendly crossed over to have a chat. Here she could also see wagons pulled by horses as they came in from the country laden with fruits and vegetables, tradesmen going to market with a hen or goose inside a sack thrown over their shoulders, and farmers' wives carrying butter and eggs for sale. It was convenient to just run out of the house and bargain for whatever she needed.

For me an added plus was the house on our left, where Rolla lived with her unmarried sister and brother. Sometimes when we sat at the kitchen table eating, Rolla's face would appear at the window, and smiling her toothless smile, she would convey how glad she was that we were now neighbors.

Remembering that sad little house in which we lived, I think of how often I wished that I could have had the kind of home many people all over the world enjoy, where they were born and in which they lived for a time, and where they return periodically for visits with the family, a place where they can find comfort whenever they need it—a refuge.

I remember our apartment in Katowice without emotion. It was a rented place in a city to which we were not allowed to return. Dabrowa was different. I was born in one of Grandmother's beds, in her home, which I grew to love. Even though almost immediately after birth, I was taken to Katowice, where my parents apparently had already lived before my sister's death, very few years later we were again living in Dabrowa for what seemed like the foreseeable future. The conscious years of my childhood were spent in Dabrowa, my childhood landscape, and despite the horrors experienced there, I continue to feel ties to that town, even after all these years. My roots are in Dabrowa.

At that time of life, I did not think of homes as objects of attachment. Newfound freedoms and friends were what mattered most. But I had a special sense of belonging in Grandmother's house. I liked its atmosphere, and the people who lived in it. I know that if my life had been the kind of life others call normal, I would have returned to Grandmother's house for as long as she was alive and even after she was gone.

During the war, when things became so hopeless that no one expected to survive, Grandmother put my name on the title to her house, hoping that I, as the youngest member of the family, would somehow manage to survive and that the house which had witnessed so much of our family's history would remain in our hands. I never went back to claim it. Newspaper and television reports of anti-Semitism in Poland today make it doubtful that I would find comfort or feel safe were I to return to any of the homes in Dabrowa to which I have some claims—Grandmother's, Father's, Aunt Raisa's, or even the little witch's house—instead I find refuge in these reminiscences.

There was also Father's parents' old home up on the hill, surrounded by that endless orchard and the mysterious ruins. Never having lived in that house, I felt only a slight sense of proprietorship there. After the Germans moved on and vacated the building, which they occupied when they took Dabrowa, it was divided into small apartments. Many strangers inhabited it. Aunt Haika and her family were the only people I knew there. But the grounds where I had spent countless happy hours left me to this day with nostalgic longing. I ate the fruit I picked while sitting on the branch of a tree. We had plums, cherries, apples, and pears.

Our last home in Dabrowa was not the kind of place one got to love. Even if we had been allowed to live there long enough to get used to it, I doubt that any of us would have been satisfied to call it home. I came, in fact, to resent the witch's house, with its cramped spaces and gloom. In moments of rebelliousness, I blamed my parents for our circumstances. At those times, Mother would ignore me by remaining silent, but Father tried patiently to explain that the house was only a stopover. Had I known that when losing that house, I would also lose my parents, I would gladly have accepted that last house as a cherished home where my parents could grow old and I could grow to maturity.

Eight

I draw boundless pleasure from nature. This emotion has its roots in the pastoral setting of Dabrowa. Here, where I had more freedom, where life was more natural and unhampered than in Katowice, I developed an affinity with the magnificent Polish forests and the rolling green landscapes around the small town. Here, after a clear summer day, I could lie in a glade and observe the sky after sunset turn the color of lemon. Here, I could also observe how at different times of day, the sun washed the land in different hues: soft and velvety in the morning like the petals of roses; white and blinding at noon; orangey and mellow in the afternoon—warm and comforting.

I also watched how the land spoke of different things at different seasons, welcoming spring as new growth filled in bare spaces, cushioning and softening the landscape. And how the sunnier heat healed scars left behind by winter. Then came favorite fall with its fullness, its bounty already heralding the hard and forbidding Polish winter and its early frosts.

I might have lived my entire life in Katowice and never have had those idyllic moments I experienced in little rustic Dabrowa. It was a world of discovery—the kind of discovery that appealed to my solitary nature. What joy I derived from Father's orchard. The fragrance of fallen fruit; plums and apples ripening on the trees because there was no one to pick them. To this day, whenever I buy plums, I think of "the orchard." The feelings of desolation that had troubled me in Katowice disappeared.

News from Father continued in the same vein. He was closing up the factory and shipping a trainload of wool to Dabrowa, and Mother, thinking out loud, often asked, "Where will he store all this wool?" Considering how expensive an ounce of wool got to be, she calculated that with the ton Father was sending, we would live in comfort for the rest of the war and have enough left to start anew when the war ended.

It was fall, and the time to start school had long passed, but the school building was occupied, and children stayed home. Two tutors from Krakow, who had settled in Dabrowa for the war, began teaching privately. One of the tutors was a man named Teufel ("devil" in German), and those who did not take lessons from him called his students devils. I don't remember my teacher's name, but I do remember what she looked like: slight of stature, with dark hair severely pulled back in a chignon, making her look stern. I suspected the purpose for that look was to maintain discipline and conceal her soft nature, but I did not have the courage to test my theory.

The schools were in the sitting room in each teacher's apartment. The room where I attended was a Victorian-looking place, somewhat dark, with velvet drapery that was perennially closed. Teacher thought that a view from the window would distract us. My class had five students, including me. The teachers thought that teaching almost on a one-on-one basis would make up for the lack of better facilities and more varied materials.

Few parents could afford to send their children to private school. Zela and Moniek did not enroll because they were preparing to go back to Katowice regardless of what might happen along the way or in Katowice itself. Aunt Gusta found her life in Dabrowa, away from her husband, unbearable.

Mother enrolled me, and for the next two and a half years, winter and summer, year-round to make up for any time lost to the war, I went to school every day, except Saturdays, with about two dozen other children, to be taught those subjects a child of my age commonly learned—except history and geography. These two subjects were forbidden by the Germans. Instead, a foreign language was offered. It was, of course, German because the tutors were afraid to teach anything else. I learned Gothic script and wrote one-page stories in that angular alphabet, enjoying my newly acquired skill.

The atmosphere in our little school was elitist. Books were advanced, possibly because they were the only ones the teachers were able to obtain. We also learned music and art, and competition among the students was fierce. Those who had Mr. Teufel felt that their course was more difficult because he was more demanding. Many heated discussions were held over this.

In my mind's eye, I still see neatly filled notebooks in well-formed handwriting, here and there an ink stain when I unconsciously dipped the pen too deeply in the inkwell. I did well in school, and whenever Mother was called in to discuss my progress, she would leave with glowing cheeks. On those days, she would stop at a friend's house, where over tea she would excitedly tell what a smart daughter she had. I was not supposed to hear any of this, but I somehow managed to hear every word.

I made a few casual friends at school, and when summer came, we met in some grassy lot two or three afternoons each week to talk and to play. We were all mature beyond our years, discussing politics and whatever books were available to us. We talked about the war and the chances of it ending soon. We even suggested plans for how to get out of Poland, which we knew was almost impossible to accomplish because we were being watched every moment. Jews were not allowed to travel, and eventually the Germans made us wear a yellow Star of David armband to make us easily identifiable. We all felt boxed in. And that was what we mostly talked about, but not always. We also took walks and played ball and discussed the books we read.

As much as I loved the summers, with their abundance of birds, flowers and berries, rolling hills and fragrant woods, I remember the winters with my friends most nostalgically: skating on the river by the railroad station, where the river was broadest, or sledding in my grandparents' orchard, where some of the hills were meters long and steep, our faces red from the cold as we sped down the slopes, laughing and shouting with joy—the joy of being alive. I felt a carefree, happy first consciousness that life was worth living, the war and our difficult circumstances momentarily forgotten. I began to cherish the topography of Father's property early in life. Picking violets in back of the house in early spring, and in the summer, climbing the fruit trees below, in the orchard, to pick fruit. I was sorry that my grandparents were no longer alive because they would have loved having us play in their garden. They would have no doubt added even more interest to the orchard than was already there.

In winter we met in Alfred's house, a long, gray structure in a fancy part of town, with a garden running alongside it. Alfred was a Teufel student, tall and thin, with black hair and very white skin. He and the other boys who sought to be friendly with some of my girlfriends and me were a little older than the girls in our group. Most of the girls took turns having a crush on Alfred. His manners were faultless, his clothing elegant; he was intelligent and had distinguished good looks. His family were assimilated Jews living like Christians.

I first met Alfred when Mother and I visited his paralyzed father, with whom Mother had gone to school. All he said that afternoon was "I am pleased," which is the conventional Polish reply to an introduction. Some weeks later, when in school he asked me to come play ball with him and his friends, I was quite surprised because I didn't think he had remembered me.

This group of friends were all (except Alfred) recent arrivals from other cities, hoping to wait out the war in Dabrowa. After my cousins left to go back to Katowice, I had made only a few casual friends at school. The day Alfred asked me to play, I flew home to tell Mother, who showed her pleasure in a broad smile.

Alfred provided many luxuries: his spacious house and garden, a sleigh with a pair of horses in winter, and a sled long enough to seat about six of us. But best of all was his complete knowledge of the town and surrounding countryside, with its many secret places for us to explore. He knew where the river passed, and he could walk alongside it for many kilometers without getting lost.

We spent summer afternoons at a swimming hole in a wooded area in the eastern part of town. The water there was calm, deep, slow moving, and so clear that the rocky bottom was visible when dappled sunshine played on its surface. There, on either side of the river, rose banks overgrown with dense shrubbery made it difficult to climb in and out of the water. We used exposed tree roots as steps and supports. I generally preferred to sit on the edge because I didn't swim. Swarms of colorful flying insects would swirl around us, butterflies so tame they settled on arms and could be observed at leisure. All this was new and exciting to those of us who had lived in cities before coming to Dabrowa.

Alfred had his crushes too. Having a large choice, he picked his girls one after another, always preferring one over the rest for a while and then changing to the next one. When the time came for his attention to center on me, I was not surprised. As I watched his behavior, I came to expect it. But the first time he threw the ball that special way at my chest, and when out of the corner of his mouth came that faint grin, I forgot everything for an instant, and I was only conscious of a special thrill and the blush I knew covered my face.

For a number of months (or was it only weeks?) after that, I became the girl for whom Alfred planned everything. This filled me with a peculiar mixture of pride and embarrassment. Secretly I was proud, and outwardly I was embarrassed. I think I was too young, not ready to be paired with a boy. I wanted to remain unfettered.

Not that Alfred was demonstratively affectionate. On the contrary, he showed his preference in an impersonal, even rough manner, by touching me lightly as he passed or by pulling my braids. But everyone in the group knew this, and there was no doubt in anyone's mind whom Alfred liked.

At that time, I developed a very close friendship with Stella, who came to mean more to me than any other friend. She lived with her mother in a wing of Alfred's house. Her mother was related to Alfred's mother, and they, too, were newcomers from Krakow, here for the duration of the war. Afternoons we did German homework together until it got so dark that lamps had to be lit and I had to go home. I always thought Stella to be smarter than I, and I told her so. She was a sensitive, thoughtful student. We discussed the subjects we were studying and compared grades we had received, but I found comparing grades distasteful when I detected a loss of interest on her part whenever my grade was higher than hers. Comparing grades threatened to put a wedge in our friendship.

After several months, Stella and I had a quarrel and stopped speaking. Days passed during which I suffered. Mother saw my pain, and it troubled her, but I was not ready to discuss it. Stella was proud, and so was I. We both knew that we must make up, but neither of us wanted to make the first move. One afternoon when I came home from school in a particularly depressed mood, Mother asked why, if I didn't want to be the first to talk to Stella, didn't I write her a note? It embarrassed me to hear Mother speak so suddenly and openly about my feelings. At the same time, I felt relieved that the ice was broken and that I could discuss my problem with someone as wise as Mother. I said I would be lowering myself in Stella's eyes if I were to make the first move. Mother had an answer for that too, saying that pride is the biggest obstacle to people's happiness.

All that afternoon I kept thinking about writing the note, and toward evening, I wrote a neat little letter, folded it many times so that the content could not be seen, and left the house.

As I neared Stella's house, I picked a boy off the street and sent him with the note while I waited behind a building for an answer. A few minutes later, the boy came running back with no note in his hand, which was a good sign because I had asked her to meet me if she wanted to make up. I left the building behind which I had been hiding and walked out into the street. From the other end came Stella, smiling as she quickened her step. I still see her face and feel the thrill as we shook hands.

After the luxurious surroundings at Alfred's house, I did not like coming home and many times went to Grandmother's instead. Mother did not make an issue of this but went about making the little witch's house as beautiful as she could. Beds were made up with hand-embroidered linens, and the table in the back room was covered with a sumptuous tablecloth of red wool with Persian designs. A collection of various pots and pans were hung around the kitchen, and the built-in table was scrubbed until the grain in the wood stood out starkly. Mother put sackcloth rags on the freshly scrubbed floors so that mud stuck to shoes would not dirty them. Gradually I got used to our nest, consoling myself that none of the other new arrivals could boast a better home.

Shortly after we were settled, Father arrived and told of the difficulties he'd had securing a freight car in Sosnowiec for shipping the wool from the factory to Dabrowa. None of the old railroad schedules applied; things were in chaos. But the wool was now well on its way, and all we had to do was wait for it to arrive.

We would live worry-free lives, Father assured us, once the wool was in our possession. Father also told us he had let Bronia go (she had come back to take care of Father while Mother and I were in Dabrowa), and he promised to hire her back after our return to Katowice. We never saw her again.

Nine

After a relative evenness in our lives, things began to change. One cold winter morning, the town was surrounded by armed Germans. Germans were on every street where Jews lived. Loudspeakers began to blast orders for everyone to stay indoors. Then the plunder began. Pushing their way into homes in pairs, they shoved people out of the way while throwing clothing out of closets and other objects all about. The announcement said they were looking for hidden weapons, but not a single weapon was found. Instead, they took silver, money, jewelry, and anything else of value they could find.

This occurrence sobered us enough to realize that nothing we possessed was safe. Mother gave her pearls, various gold pieces, and most of her jewelry to Grandmother, who collected her own and Aunt Franka's jewelry as well. Together they dug a deep hole in Grandmother's courtyard, where in an aluminum pot they buried these valuables for future use. The hiding places they had used until now no longer seemed safe. "They may someday have to be exchanged for food," Grandmother said. My family never got a chance to dig up the pot. It was left where it was buried.

People were showing fear in various other ways; services in the synagogue were shortened, and the men no longer sang after Friday night services. Jews tried to be invisible. They did not want to draw attention to themselves. New laws that narrowed our lives were being put into effect successively until we became virtual prisoners.

On Saturdays after lunch, no one in Dabrowa worked, and most people were taking naps. Thus the town was quiet, and the trucks that roared into the market roused us abruptly into a paralyzing fear. Dozens of soldiers surrounded the most heavily populated streets and began another search. This time the search was for fur. Over blaring loudspeakers, they informed us all to bring out our furs for collection. No one would be allowed to keep any fur, not even trimmings on coats or hats. Large barrels were set up every few feet on each street corner, and with each knock on a door, another barrel was filled with fur.

In Poland, where winters are long and cold, fur around the neck, as a head covering, or lining a coat was a necessity. Nearly everyone, no matter how poor, managed to have a fur collar on a winter coat or even a pair of fur-lined boots. So the Germans collected quite a bit of fur even though it may not have been the best or the most expensive kind.

The fur collection was serious because it left many people without important winter clothing, and replacements could not be bought—for the moment, Dabrowa was stripped of all fur. Fabrics, especially woolens, were also not available. Eventually, a black market in good used winter clothes was operating. Some of the refugees from large cities, who had settled in Dabrowa for safety, were selling their clothes to buy food, but prices were high, and such clothing had to be altered in most cases. The best customers were farmers who brought in butter, chickens, and other staples. They ended up with these fine things.

In this systematic way, we were stripped not only of freedom, but of all those things that made survival possible. Mother's friend who was married to the dentist visited and offered to take any fur to hide it because she lived in a Christian neighborhood, where furs were not collected, but it was too late. Mother had already given up ours.

Following the fur collection, bills were posted all over town that anyone found wearing or hiding fur would be put in jail,

Christians excluded. Later, when snow fell, people wore their cloth coats, and devoid of any fur, they somehow looked as if they were not fully dressed.

We were given something in its place—a yellow Star of David armband to wear on the left arm. At the same time, a 9:00 p.m. curfew was imposed on Jews, who were to be off the streets. Children below the age of twelve were exempt. Failure to comply with that law was punishable by a fine and jail.

At first the Star of David seemed like a joke, and no one minded it. After all, we all knew who we were, and everyone else knew who we were too. But after a while, it became clear what a handicap this armband was since Jews had been restricted from going on trains and from traveling altogether. Before the armband ordinance, many had continued to travel; now with this glaring identification on the arm, most were afraid to take the chance. To leave the house without the band on the left arm, after having worn it for some time, created such fear in people that hardly anyone tried it. Yet, there were those who did, especially those who did not resemble the stereotypical description of what Jews were supposed to look like.

What did a Jew look like? Every caricature showed him to be short and fat, with dark hair and dark eyes, and, of course, every Jew had a big nose. How many people the world over answer to this description, people who have never been in contact with Jews and who would not recognize a Jew as being different because of the similarity to their own race? And what about all those Jews who did not look like the advertised cartoon character?

Yes, some people took chances; they traveled without the armband and got away with it. Others got caught and were fined and thrown in jail.

Again and again, one must wonder at the indomitability of the human spirit. Much later, when we were allowed to inhabit only two streets in town (the ghetto), and the rooms in which we all lived could barely hold all of us, some individuals still had enough energy and motivation to be entrepreneurs. So strong was the desire to live that even in the most degrading circumstances, we still had hope of a future. A man whose house had a large shady tree in front of it seized the opportunity on hot sunny days to charge a fee for the privilege of a half hour's respite under his tree. His business consisted of a tree and a chair, and his job was to keep track of the time. He had customers. To sit in the shade on a sunny day, away from a crowded apartment, was luxury.

In some small ways, life seemed to take on a regular routine: the farmers brought their food to town, and women bought and cooked. Mindy continued to work on wigs because there was a steady demand, and Dolores was seen on the street with her ever-present basket looped over her arm.

* * *

Many weeks had passed since Father's arrival from Katowice, but there was still no sign of the wool he'd sent. Father also had a long list of accounts that owed him money, and I could tell from their conversations that Mother was angling for a trip to Katowice, and Father was ready to give in. They decided that she would go and try to collect some of the outstanding debts in Father's books. This meant traveling deeper into the Third Reich because Katowice was now annexed to Germany—it was also Judenfrei. Mother seemed not to give all this any thought. "Just give me the book, Joske, and tell me a little about what these people are like," she said.

As soon as the decision was made, she packed some clothing, and the following morning, by herself, without the Star of David armband, she left for the railroad station. She later told us that when our neighborhood was behind her, she hailed a fiacre and rode to the station in style. Father and I saw her off then walked home with pounding hearts. We did not speak. During that period in our lives, neither Mother nor Father showed when they were profoundly moved, and living with them, I learned to keep emotions in check. Risk taking became a part of our daily lives; there was hardly any need to discuss it.

During Mother's absence, Father and I kept house, but neither of us knew anything about cooking. I remember boiling potatoes with too much salt—we ate them anyway. Of course, our daily topic was Mother's safety and our longing to have her back home. She was gone a week, and when she came back, she told us how comfortably she had traveled, and how when she got to Katowice, soldiers at a checkpoint were demanding identification from all travelers. Reading her name, Ita Kamm (pronounced "Eeda" in German), they took her to be at least part German, which she did not deny. She was asked where she was from, and she said Tarnów. She didn't know how much these soldiers knew about Dabrowa, and she found it safer to name a larger city, where the population was more diverse. She was also asked why she was visiting Katowice, to which she replied, without skipping a beat, that she was visiting her sister who lives there. With that, they waved her on.

Sitting around the large table in our sitting room, we listened to her for hours describing every detail of her trip and her feelings about what was going on with Father's business associates, who were, of course, Christians and therefore still in business. They were amazed to see Mother collecting bills. Some were kind and generous, but others refused to pay "at this time" because, they said, "business is nonexistent, and we need to make rent."

Mother talked into the night, saying that Katowice was not recognizable: streets were deserted; many apartments stood empty. She had stayed in a guesthouse, afraid to go to our apartment, where people knew her. She did not see Aunt Gusta and her family; she didn't know if they were in their home, and she did not try to find them for fear of being discovered and of endangering them as well as herself.

Father and I were too happy for words to have her back safely and so proud of her accomplishment. We were also happy about the leather satchel full of money she brought. "How much will you give me for this?" she asked him before handing it over. With a broad grin, he answered, "All of it. It's all yours." Seeing them together, laughing, I had a—now rare—feeling of well-being. Mother, Father, money to buy food with. . . . In the days that followed, we settled into a routine of three meals a day, school for me until one o'clock in the afternoon, then play with friends and evenings at home. The three of us, Mother, Father and I, lived a closer, more intimate life than ever before. Father now had unlimited time. Such small economic activity as was possible was not in Father's line, so his chief occupation was visiting certain friends and mainly his younger brother, Meyer, who still kept a stable of horses. At times he went, like Uncle Emil, to the confectionary for a soda and to talk to the people who gathered there.

We had no servants to disturb our privacy, and the house was so small that we were always within each other's sight. There were no movies or restaurants to go to, and once Mother's housework was done, she could sit with me or with Father and talk. I provided a good deal of entertainment with stories of my friends and of happenings at school. Father would describe the various horses Uncle Meyer had bought, sold, or traded. Sometimes Uncle Emil and Aunt Franka would come to visit, but mostly we visited them. Our house did not lend itself to company—it was dark and small. Grandmother's home was grand by comparison.

Mother was now occupied with and interested in different things than she had been in Katowice. Her readings were now limited because she could get only novels that made the rounds among her friends; no other books were available. There were no newspapers, and learning English was out of the question; I cannot even imagine the kind of punishment one would have gotten if caught learning English. She was busy baking bread, washing clothes by hand, and scrubbing floors. I was surprised when I first saw her doing these things. I knew my Mother to be well groomed, sitting with her embroidery basket, reading or cooking. Now I often found her in front of a tub of steaming, soapy water, scrubbing sheets against the washboard. After she learned to climb proficiently through the back window, she would hang the laundry in our tiny courtyard. She was as efficient in these tasks as she had been in everything she did in Katowice.

In winter the laundry was hung in the kitchen, where the built-in stove glowed hot while bread was baking and soup bubbled on top of it. Whatever she did always turned out wonderfully. The sheets were immaculate, the bread delicious, an occasional cake a delicacy. Mother usually baked several of her dark pumpernickel loaves at one time. When the bread was fresh, it was crisp and fragrant, and we could easily finish a whole loaf for supper. Of course we did not have much to go with it—butter, a scrambled egg, which had always been my least favorite food but which had suddenly become much loved. My lack of appetite from early childhood was gone. Now I could not get my fill of food. I found everything to be delicious, and fresh-laid eggs became a delicacy. Mother often teased that if she had known I would develop such an appetite during a war, when food was scarce, she might have prayed for war years ago.

If we were rendered humble by our modest lifestyle, no one would have known it. I heard no complaints from either of my parents. The simplicity of our existence, spiced occasionally with an unexpected visitor or the purchase on the black market of a jar of preserves, was enough to satisfy us. We knew this, and we frequently spoke about it. There was only one thing we longed for—to be left alone by the Germans.

Certain things we found out about our house kept us in stitches for days. We seemed to have an attic about which we knew nothing until a neighbor explained that the ladder in our courtyard, leaning against the upper part of the building, was used to go up to the attic that belonged to our house. However, to reach our courtyard, we had to go through Rolla's house, the back of which led to the courtyard fence. The only other way to reach the ladder was through our back room window.

Mother at once discounted going through Rolla's house because it would have meant disturbing that family. Going through the window was easy for me, but Mother, who was tall and who, I am sure, had never climbed through windows in her life, had difficulty at first. She tried different ways of sitting on the ledge then swinging both legs over it—that did not work. The window space was too small for her. Finally, she tried placing one leg over the window sill, letting it dangle down into the courtyard, then swinging the other leg over the window ledge and jumping down. In due course, Mother became good at this, and it would take her only a few seconds to do it. The first time she accomplished this was one of those days when she allowed herself to be happy, and we spent much time laughing while this maneuver was going on. When Father got home that afternoon, we told him of our discovery, to which he responded by climbing nimbly out the window to inspect our newfound territory.

Looking around the dark attic, candle in hand and me in tow, he called down to Mother ecstatically, "The attic is as large as our entire house. We can use it for storage and as a hiding place if need be." "What do you mean as a hiding place?" I asked, at once alert. "Nothing. I thought, just in case. . . ." He didn't want to frighten me.

We spent so much time examining the attic and talking about it that day that Mother didn't bother to prepare supper—we ate bread and drank coffee. Our coffee was made of roasted chicory root, not of coffee beans as most people know it today. No real coffee was available to us during the war. The food didn't matter. Our attic adventure and the acquisition of additional space was worth the small sacrifice.

A few days later, Mother asked Father to line the attic floor with straw because she intended to keep chickens there. Soon a pair of hens clucked happily over our heads, and after a while, Mother was taking care of a flock of eight. We now had not only our own poultry, but also fresh eggs, and Mother proudly considered herself a farmer, though I know she would have given it up in a minute had she had the choice.

As part of the furniture in our sitting and sleeping room were two large trunks for storage. The larger of the two was the black one, which sat on four rather large wheels, the trunk Mother had filled with some of our fine things and sent to Grandmother before we fled Katowice. Mother called the trunk bewitched. It held several trays separated by plywood sheets, and she could never quite figure out how many divisions there were. Sometimes she was able to open only the top two compartments. At other times, out of the blue, another one or two would swing open. When she mostly used the two upper trays, the others shut themselves off, and a trick was required to open them. In this black trunk, Mother stored our fine linen and new clothing, which was becoming more precious with each passing season. It was better capital than money because it was a sought-after commodity that could at any time be exchanged for food.

The other, smaller trunk was brown, and it stood flat on its bottom. In that trunk we stored our food provisions: flour, sugar, barley, beans. Mice enjoyed these provisions as much as we did.

Once, after a particularly noisy night, Mother went hunting near the trunk and found a large nest of newborn mice. Naked, helpless, and squealing, their mother was not around. Mother picked them up on her dustpan and with one vigorous toss, threw the lot out the front door, into the mud on the street, where they soon disappeared under horses' hoofs. As if it were something she encountered every day, Mother didn't even bother to talk about it.

This was not a laughing matter—our food supply was in jeopardy. Since every bad thing is counterbalanced by something good, that incident brought the fulfillment of one of my heart's desires: we got a cat. The cat turned out to be a wonderful hunter; within a few weeks, when all the mice were gone, her job done, she simply disappeared, never to be seen or heard of again.

At another time, Father came home with his shoulder ripped open and bleeding. He and his brother Meyer had tried to break a young filly, hoping to sell her for a good price on Friday's market. But the horse had different ideas. She embedded her teeth in the flesh of Father's shoulder, leaving him wounded and bleeding. Mother caught sight of him being brought home and ran to remove his coat and shirt. When she saw an outline of the horse's teeth on each side of his shoulder, she cried out, frightened, and sent me across the street to Grandmother's for help. Grandmother greeted me as usual with a smile, ready for a hug, but she stopped when I called, "Grandmother, come quickly. Father has been wounded and is bleeding terribly. Mother sent me for your help. Please hurry. Don't wait!"

Grandmother grabbed a white sheet out of her closet and threw it to Aunt Franka as they ran across the street. "Tear this sheet into even-sized bandages," she ordered. To me, she said, "Sala, I have a tea kettle with water on the stove. Wait for the water to heat, then call one of us to pick it up." And to Mother, "Irena, use the iodine after you have cleaned the wound thoroughly." Each of us obeyed without complaint. Everyone was serious and worried, but Father, with his perennial good nature, managed a few smiles while he told us how it happened and how Meyer had struggled to free him from the horse's grip. Mother reprimanded him for lack of care for his safety, and Grandmother ordered a glass of slivovitz, a plum brandy, to deaden the pain. While he drank, he spoke dreamily, "She has a bad temper. Meyer better sell her on Friday before she harms someone else." From that day for about a week, Father was clucked over by all of us until the wound showed that it was healing.

Some weeks passed quietly. The Germans kept to themselves, but there was a general feeling that something bad was about to happen. Panic stricken for the safety of all of us, Father wanted to visit Warsaw again to see what, if anything, could be done to speed up the process of our emigration to America. Shortly before the outbreak of war, when he had inquired about the status of our application, he had been told that we would have to wait for our number to be called. Thus, in the early years of war, we still thought—hoped—we had a chance to be called. Mother, however, discouraged him from making this trip, fearing that out of the many people he knew there, someone night denounce him for traveling without an armband. She also reasoned that since Jews were not allowed to travel, we would probably not be allowed to leave the country even if our number did come up. Father, she thought, would be taking an unnecessary risk. "Don't go, Joske." He did not go.

Ten

W hen I was free of schoolwork, Mother sometimes took me with her when she visited her friend Rachel. Rachel had two sons: Moniek, who was twenty-one years old at the time, and William, whom we called Vovek, who was seventeen. The younger brother usually entertained me with his jokes and on the harmonica while our mothers drank tea. Vovek was handsome, and he played love songs on the harmonica—I was fascinated by his charm and his skill. It wasn't long before he began visiting me. My parents did not like this, and they made it clear that he was to limit his visits. Stung by the rebuff, he stopped coming by altogether. (He survived the war and we met perchance on a New York City street in 1950. He showed me the number tattooed on his arm in Auschwitz and described some of the tortures he experienced in three other concentration camps. But that is another story.)

After one of our visits to Rachel's, Mother was particularly quiet. That evening at supper, she told Father to go out to the country first thing in the morning because the Germans were planning to close the town again and take hundreds of men for forced labor.

"Who told you that?" Father asked.

"Rachel."

Father agreed to leave at dawn, but he did not make it. At about three the following morning, a shouting arose on the street, and when Father went to answer the pounding on the door, two Germans—pistols in hand—stood there ready to take him. He barely had time to slip into his clothes and glance in our direction. (Mother and I cowered in bed not wanting to be seen.) Rachel's husband and her older son, Moniek, were also taken that morning, as was our friend the dentist. But only Father was taken in our family. Vovek had escaped by leaving for the country the evening before.

Wasting no time, Mother and I dressed immediately after Father's departure, and when the shouting and commotion on the street stopped, we went out to the square. It was now daylight, and an icy wind lashed about our heads. Assembled in the square were hundreds of men, huddled together in groups, many without coats, some in their nightshirts, waiting for the trucks, which were just arriving to take them away.

Women of all ages were standing around crying, wailing, calling out to their loved ones, "Button your coat. Here take this sweater. I brought your hat!" And the men, bewildered and speechless, did as they were told. The Germans meanwhile stood around talking and joking among themselves and directing the men not to leave their group, shoving them back into place with loaded pistols. Finally, the men were loaded on trucks, and the grief-stricken women ran after them with outstretched arms, waving goodbye as one truck after another roared away for an unknown destination. Although they collected several hundred men, they did not take all. This didn't seem to be their intention—just a taste of what was to come.

No explanation was given for why the men were taken or where. The Germans who remained in the square said they were being taken for two weeks of labor. After that, they would be back. The women were told to go home, and slowly, one by one, some in groups, they did as they were told.

When we got home, Mother took off her coat and sat down in the kitchen without speaking. There was no expression on her face; her eyes stared into the distance. She was dry eyed and pale. She did not answer my questions, and I knew not to insist, to let her be. This was a pose she would take many more times as the weeks and months passed and we were progressively stripped of the last vestiges of human dignity.

We became chattels of the Germans, who could confiscate our possessions and separate us from our families, take away our most basic freedoms without giving reasons for anything they chose to do with us and to us.

From the day he was taken, we waited for Father to return. No news came from any of the men, and days turned into weeks without a sign of life from anyone who had been taken. At meals, silent tears rolled down our cheeks and onto our plates.

In the meantime, Mother, taking over Father's duties, continued to inquire about the carload of wool. One evening when I came home from Alfred's, I found the house in darkness. As I removed my boots in the kitchen, Mother lit the lamp and looked at me in my drenched coat. She looked even more gray than usual, and pointing to the table, she muttered something about the railroad office. I read the note: "The carload of wool shipped from Sosnowiec has not arrived here, and we regret to inform you that it is believed to be lost." I ran to Mother and buried my head in her chest, shaking with sobs. She hugged me tightly and put her face down on my head. We stood like this until I stopped crying. Then she took me by the hand and said we would have fresh scrambled eggs for supper.

After the dishes were washed, she blew out the lamp to save kerosene, and we sat in front of the kitchen window in darkness, looking at the deserted street. Outside, the wind howled and torrents of rain beat against the house. As we stared into the blackness, I perceived Mother's aged profile. I felt terribly sad because I was helpless, and I so wanted to help her. That night in bed, I was full of worry and loneliness. I thought of my attacks of fear in Katowice, and of the reality that now faced me each day, and how this reality provided enough worry, leaving no room for imagined dangers, and I cried myself to sleep.

A few days later, coming home from school, I saw Father coming to meet me from the opposite direction. He was waving and laughing. I ran into his open arms, not believing what was happening. He had arrived mid-morning and decided to meet me as I walked home for lunch. At home, Mother had dinner ready, and as we sat down together, we could not contain tears of happiness for being reunited. Father told us how the trucks had taken them to an unknown place, where they were housed in flimsy barracks without light or plumbing. They lived all this time in the same clothing they had worn when they were taken as no work clothes were given them. The food was rationed out twice daily: in the morning, before they left for work, and at night, after they returned. The men were divided into groups and taken to different job sites. Father worked on building a road; others worked in garages, cleaning and repairing trucks and other war machinery; and those who were too old or too frail to work were taken away in trucks guarded by armed soldiers, and no one knew where they were sent.

He said he started planning his escape as soon as he was certain of the daily routine. At the end of each workday, the men were given a five-minute break to relieve themselves in the bushes. Father looked for a secluded spot, lay down flat underneath the scrub when he first got there, and remained so until everyone was gone. When the men were loaded back on the truck in the dark, his absence was not detected. Later, removing the armband, he walked to the first farmhouse, where he saw a light. There he asked if he could spend the night in the barn. Eyeing him suspiciously, the farmer grudgingly granted his request. Early next morning, when it was still dark and Father tried to leave the barn unseen, the farmer surprised him with a thick slice of bread and told him where he was. They had been taken to Gorlice—a good distance away from Tarnów—where the Germans had repair shops and where they had to build better roads for access to their shops.

At first Father pretended that he knew perfectly well where he was, but seeing that the farmer meant no harm, he gave in, and although he did not admit that he was Jewish, he allowed the farmer to drive him to the nearest railroad station, which turned out to be in Gorlice. With the money that he of late had permanently sewn into his coat lining, he was able to buy a ticket to Tarnów, and from there he walked to Dabrowa, hitching rides on passing wagons.

His experiences made us want to take care of Father, to pamper him. Mother heated water, and the big wooden tub was set up in the middle of the back room. I was asked to visit Grandmother while Father bathed and changed into fresh clothes.

Many wives and mothers came to inquire about the men who had been taken with Father, and we worried that someone would denounce him to the Germans for having escaped. It was becoming common knowledge that some people were working for the Germans, spying on what was happening in town. I wonder what kind of desperation drives people to commit such acts? On the other hand, there were those who worked for the Germans but brought to the attention of the town things they overheard while doing their clerical or cleaning duties, such as news of an impending act against the Jews. We were sometimes alerted by those people a day or two before the event happened, and some lives were saved that way, although not for long. As one heinous act followed another, those who were saved once would give their lives the next time.

No one denounced Father. In fact, soon after, a number of the other men who had been taken began quietly reappearing.

In the weeks that followed, the only flaw in our domestic happiness was that there was no income. Father made various efforts to get in touch with the retailers whom he had supplied with merchandise from his factory. Many of these businesses were owned by Christians and were therefore still in operation. The response to his efforts was minimal, and Mother began selling some of the clothing from the black trunk: coats, suits, fine linens, sheer stockings. At first she sold the items that were getting too small for me. Then came the clothes Mother thought would be out of style by war's end and finally everything that was worth selling. But she always saved certain things for "when we return." We ate well during those months because she sold to farmers who paid with food, and she continued to raise her chickens.

Our lives were so precarious that even this simple way of survival would be denied us. News from neighboring towns and cities became very discouraging. Germans were killing Jews on the streets in broad daylight at close range—but the worst shootings occurred at night. At first this did not ring true. We did not believe these stories until one night, in the quiet of predawn hours, we could hear shots from Tarnów. Next morning, news reached us that nearly five hundred people had been massacred—men, women, and children. When what happened in Tarnów was confirmed, Dabrowa became panic stricken. We did not know which way to turn. We felt trapped. For the moment, however, the town remained untouched by that awful thing that came to be known as *akcja* (literally translated as "action"), but what had been known long ago as *pogrom*, a unilateral military assault on unarmed people.

We lived in dread of an akcja. Not knowing what was going on in other towns did not help. Such news as we got was through hearsay, and it was so awful that we hoped it wasn't true. If anyone still possessed a radio, no one knew about it because people were afraid of informants. We got to know who these informants were, and it became progressively more difficult for them to collect accurate information.

At home Mother still had her chickens; Father—the wound from the horse bite having completely healed—returned to Uncle Meyer's stable of horses; and I continued to attend school, where I excelled in (of all things) German and was promoted to a higher level. I mastered the Gothic alphabet and improved in composition writing as well as in advanced German conversation. On rare peaceful days, I played with my friends, and when alone, I philosophized and soliloquized in front of the hanging mirror above the black trunk in our back room. When bored, I visited Grandmother and Aunt Franka. There, the two uncles were rarely home. Uncle Emil usually spent his days in the confectionary shop, which was owned by Vovek's mother, Rachel. In that shop, over soda water with raspberry syrup, people gathered to discuss our situation and to make predictions based on the skimpy information they had. I was often called by Uncle Emil to come into the shop for a soda when he saw me passing it. Sometimes when he met me walking, Uncle Emil would press some change in my hand and say, "Buy yourself something," just as he had in Katowice when I was a young child.

No one knew where Uncle Herman spent his days. He had his own set of friends, most of them Christian. We didn't know where they met. From time to time, he was seen talking with Eva.

I was now seeing more of my cousin Ceska, Uncle Meyer's daughter. Our friendship had begun a few years earlier when Mother and I had spent summers in Krynica, and now we again found things in common, especially because we lived near each other and it was safer not to be seen on the street—exposure was dangerous. She and I met some afternoons in her home. There we sewed clothes and cooked meals for her dolls in discarded shoepaste tins; we recited poetry and wrote short stories. Ceska attended Mr. Teufel's classes, and she was not part of my group of friends. We were able to compare what we were learning and how good our teachers were.

Ceska had a doll-like face with full pink cheeks, cornflower blue eyes, and a tiny turned-up nose. She was mild natured, introspective, intelligent. Where I had no toys at all, and I never actually wanted any, especially since losing the gypsy man and ballerina dolls I had taken from Aunt Raisa's house (I don't remember what happened to them), Ceska had a multitude of different kinds of dolls from smallest imaginable to two feet long. Most were made of pink plastic, but some were made of rags. All of them needed to be clothed. She loved playing with dolls. Cooking food or sewing clothes for her brood was how she spent her time. When she wasn't doing that, she read. Ceska lived in a world of her own creation, a world of mystery and fantasy.

* * *

Winter in early 1941 was in its full blustering glory. In the villages, snow stretched across the fields as far as the eye could reach. In town, people walked in a maze of narrow paths between two walls of snow. Icicles, like crystal earrings, hung from roofs, rarely melting before the end of March or April. Father, and sometimes Mother, split the delicate birch logs we had stored in the kitchen for burning in our two stoves. I liked peeling the white bark off the logs and throwing it in the fire to watch it crackle and sputter as it burned.

It was a good time for sledding, and Stella, Alfred, the rest of the group, and I managed to meet at least once or twice a week. Our sled speeding furiously down the steep hill, with one of the boys in front to guide it, the rest of us sitting one behind the other, produced a kind of exhilaration difficult to describe. Nothing mattered in those moments. The road was long and steep, the snow tightly packed, and we were warm, comfortable, glad to be together, and no one bothered us. It was easy to forget how cruel reality was. The sky, the sun, the snow, youth belonged to us, and we were unreservedly happy. Afterwards, we would go to Alfred's house, where we sat around telling stories.

Sometimes a day like that coincided with Mother's feeling rich because she had sold a piece of clothing for more food than expected, and when I got home, there would be a good supper in the sitting room/bedroom on the red wool tablecloth, a blazing fire in the pot-bellied stove, and the lamp would be turned up high. On those days I considered myself the happiest girl in the world, and I would not have changed places with anyone for anything—not even with Shirley Temple, who was the only actress I knew and the envy of all girls.

But my happiness could change in an instant. One snowy evening, as I trudged home, the streets lit only by the whiteness of the snow, I was passing the apothecary's shop on the square when a group of teenage Christian girls surrounded me and demanded I give them what I had in my pockets. I had nothing, and I turned my coat pockets inside out to show them that I had nothing, which made them angry. They began pushing me from one to the other, tearing at my clothes and hitting me over the head until they tore off my hat and slapped me across the face. Having been taken by surprise, I remained silent to that point, but the sting of their slap on my icy cheek revived me. I screamed, "Why are you doing this?" Shocked by my outburst and the sudden sound of my voice, they ran, yelling back, "fucking Jewess."

I picked up my hat and, placing it carefully on my disheveled hair, started slowly down the street. I wanted some time to gain composure before reaching home. The crunch of the snow under my feet, the only sound, brought back equanimity, but the feeling of long ago, when I had first encountered anti-Semitism in a tram in Katowice, returned—the feeling of being flawed, inferior, of not being able to measure up to other people because I was Jewish. An old, almost forgotten, weight in my chest returned. I wanted to weep but dared not.

My parents never knew of this incident. Had I told them, I would not have been allowed out in the evenings, and I was not ready to relinquish that freedom.

* * *

A river winds its course around Dabrowa. It is narrow and deep in the east end of town, and it widens and becomes shallow as it proceeds down to the railroad station in the west. Here we skated. Skating on the frozen river by the railroad with many other children and young adults was one of the very few—perhaps the only—place where people congregated in such numbers at that time. No one seemed to worry about safety when we skated, but no one stayed until evening. As soon as it began to get dark, the place became deserted. As we walked back uphill, an acquaintance with a horse-drawn sleigh might give us a ride; if not, we would race back to the top, where we would part, each taking his road home.

As my outgrown clothing was being sold, I needed new things, most of all boots and a warm winter coat. New fabrics were not to be had for any price, so an old, dark blue blanket was tailored into a new coat, and my leather book bag was sacrificed for a pair of boots. My new outfit was beautiful, especially the handsewn boots, which became the envy of my friends.

Food, too, was difficult to get in winter. Flour was expensive, and butter was a luxury because many of the farmers didn't want to travel the icy roads to town. No money could buy meat or sugar, but every once in a while, a supply of marmalade would appear at some store. It was thin and dark, of uncertain ingredients, but it was sweet, and we never missed an opportunity to buy it.

Occasionally, the cold would loosen its grip for a day, giving a false impression of spring. The snow would start to melt, and the exotic flora with which frost had decorated window panes all winter would disappear. People were glad to open windows to air their homes. But this thaw would vanish as suddenly as it had appeared, and when the town refroze, it took on the bizarre look of surrealist art. From rooftops hung long ice cones, askew; walkways became dangerously frozen into jagged shapes that made them nearly impossible to traverse. And once more the town stood still, gray and unmoving, waiting for spring.

One afternoon, Alfred wanted to go to the caves because he thought that in case of severe danger, we might find shelter and safety there. These caves were apparently never visited by anyone. Whenever we met there, nothing seemed to have ever been disturbed. The floors remained strewn with broken bricks and animal bones (surely someone must have tried to live there a very long time ago). The mystery of the caves appealed to us, but I believe that the safety and privacy we felt in them were the primary reasons we met there.

Alfred's plan was not very complicated. He simply thought that we would go all the way to the end of the caves and that because it was very dark, no one would want to look for us there. What he did not take into consideration was that there was no exit. Entrance and exit were one, and if no one else would venture to the end, neither would we. On the other hand, if the Germans ever found us there, we would be shot. So that afternoon, while happy and pleasant because we always enjoyed being together, ended in disappointment.

Dabrowa II

Eleven

When I was growing up, nearly all the girls I knew kept a diary. Not all diaries were the same. Some had pretty covers on them but not too much inside. Others had meticulous notes of events that were important to the girls who kept them. Then there were those who called their diaries "journals." They made daily entries listing every detail. I didn't fall in any of these categories. The diary I kept consisted of a few abbreviated words on scraps of paper, which I kept in a self-made folder marked "to be worked on at a later time." They were meant to help me remember things of momentous import that were happening at the time. As it turned out, years later, things still stood out clearly in my memory, like photographs in an album.

One memorable day was in April 1941, a little before dawn, when the sound of a shot woke us. Other shots followed quickly. My parents jumped out of their beds, and Father, in nightclothes, went out the window and up the ladder to the attic. I remained on my cot in a corner of the room, petrified, watching this hurried maneuver. Mother very quietly began closing the window after Father's escape, but then she froze. Raising myself noiselessly on an elbow, I saw in the semidarkness outside the window two uniformed Germans moving toward our tiny courtyard, pistols in hand, ready to shoot whomever they saw. Mother stood still, unable or unwilling to move so as not to attract their attention. I felt my heart in my throat; for an interminable time, everything stopped. Mother's eyes were glued to one spot, unseeing, and I was fully conscious of the danger, my head against the wall, waiting.

A frantic thought came to me that in his haste, Father might have left the attic door open. What if a breeze were to move it, alerting the Germans to the open attic? Or what if Father hadn't pulled up the ladder after he reached the top? He couldn't possibly have remembered to do all this in the short time he had. Then I saw Mother move away from the window and collapse on her bed, clutching her stomach. From that I gathered that the Germans had gone. Meanwhile shots continued, reaching us from all directions—some with tremendous impact, indicating their proximity. An occasional scream was deadened by a shot. Then we heard a thunderous order: "Alle Juden raus!" More shots, screams mingled with German voices barking orders, shots, shots, shots, then nothing—total quiet, and the sky began to fade. The hunt was over. Satiated by their night's kill, the Germans were gone.

Without speaking and still clutching her stomach, Mother moved off her bed and walked into the kitchen to look out the window that faced the street. I followed, and what I saw left an indelible stamp on my mind. Bodies were strewn all over the street, most of them naked, some in nightclothes. Rivulets of blood curled the dust on the road. I saw the finality of death—an end, a cessation of everything. I looked at the blood-splattered, crumpled bodies and rage rose in me at the unfairness, at the savagery of this monstrous event.

Silent tears poured down my face, and Mother, seeing this, took me in her arms. As I felt her tears on my hair, a fit of sobs shook my body, and I looked up at her, sobbing out, "Why did this happen?" She shook her head, not knowing how to answer my question. I screamed angry, disjointed words. I said I wanted to run and let the wind carry my anger to the world. Pain racking my chest, I became incoherent until Mother led me back to bed. Holding my hand in hers, she spoke soothing words until we saw Father moving down the ladder from the attic.

By the time the sun had risen fully, the streets were filled with people collecting their dead, weeping and begging God for mercy. Mothers screamed as they looked at their murdered sons; wives wept over their husbands; and husbands wept over their wives. Children were throwing themselves on top of their dead parents, begging them to come back to life.

Nothing I have experienced since—except those pogroms that followed this one—has equaled the heart-rending scene that followed this first akcja.

Up the street from Grandmother's house lived a family of eleven. The oldest of the children, Shayna, a girl eighteen years old, had jumped out of bed when the shooting began and was taking off her nightgown to get dressed when a bullet, flying in through the door, struck her down. Now her mother was sitting on the front step of her house, wailing and rending her clothes, mourning her eldest daughter, her helpmate and her hope.

A number of our acquaintances lost their lives, as did one or two of my parents' close friends. Our family remained intact.

The day turned clear and warm. Before noon, horse-drawn wagons appeared, driven by Jewish militia who began to clear the dead off the streets. Bodies that had not been taken away by families were lifted and tossed like sacks of wheat on the wagons. When heaped full, the wagons proceeded to the cemetery, dropping clods of coagulated blood along the way. There a huge grave awaited the cargo, and one by one the bodies were dropped into it.

That first akcja left the town devoid of energy, and for the following few days, when everyone mourned, people moved about as if in a dream. We feared a follow-up. Uncle Emil spent the next several nights with Father in our attic. Uncle Herman went to a Christian friend on the periphery of town. Mother and I left the house only for necessities, at which times I inquired about my friends, all of whom had survived. School was closed the day following the massacre, but it opened the morning after that. I don't remember if anyone attended—I did not. A few people tried to resume their normal activities, but they were not successful because they were in the minority. Every family was in one way or another touched by what had happened.

The Germans gave no explanation for what they had done; in fact, other than hushed discussions in family circles, no one spoke openly about that April day. A pall hung over our town as we tried to make sense of our lives. The religious wondered if we were being punished for past sins, but even they could find no justification for such cruel punishment. Others thought that informants among us were to blame, but no clear explanation could be reached in our search for a cause for this tragedy. In time, we got used to the idea that there was no reason other than the Germans' desire to wipe the Jews off the face of the earth. We now had concrete proof that what we were told had been happening in other towns was indeed true.

In addition to being afraid of the Germans, many people began fearing the Jewish militia (an auxiliary to the Polish police and the German army, recruited by the Germans to do the dirty work for them), who in some instances exercised their power to push the rest of us around. But as it eventually turned out, the duties of the militia were primarily to clean up the town after each akcja, even though some of those recruited seemed better disposed toward the Germans than toward their fellow Jews. There were a few who seemed prepared to do anything for the Germans, thinking they would save their lives by ingratiating themselves and giving the Germans information to help them in the plans they had for us.

It is frightening how people's minds can be turned from everything they know and supposedly love—their culture, their beliefs, their family—to such complete betrayal by deluding themselves that they would thus be saved from persecution and death. Most of the militia, though interested in saving themselves, would not sell out to the Germans. Yet, the two or three who did caused the public to be suspicious of them all. In the end, not one militiaman was saved, because once their work was done, they too were "exterminated." There was nothing left for them to do. They were the last ones to be shot or, in some cases, to be sent to concentration camps.

We slept fully clothed, as if it would make a difference whether we got shot fully dressed or in nightclothes. We felt that being dressed, we were ready to run. Where? No one could answer that.

At this time, I began thinking seriously about God. I had not been taught religion formally. What I knew about it was from observing Mother keep a kosher home and seeing my parents go to synagogue on holidays. I remembered Grandfather as a respected religious figure, and I knew that my family were observing Jews. I accepted all this as a matter of course without being particularly conscious of a higher deity presiding over our lives. Thus, when I heard the mourners ask God for mercy or ask why He allowed such an atrocity, it dawned on me that He might not exist, or that if He did exist, He had forgotten us. I wanted to cry, but no tears came. I wanted someone to reassure me, to tell me that what happened had all been a dreadful mistake and that it would never happen again. But no one did, and no one could give me this kind of comfort.

Another akcja did not follow right away, and gradually life took on a normal pace again. Looking back at those days, I am amazed at the speed with which the mind is capable of burying experiences. We were already conditioned to our inhuman circumstances. Food and clothing became once more the occupying thought of the moment—that is, until an epidemic of typhoid fever broke out. Rumor had it that German spies injected typhoid germs into milk before it was distributed for Jewish consumption. We stopped buying milk for a while. More reliable was a fact that many witnessed, including me: a civilian spilling boxes of contaminated metal nibs for pens into the curbs on all streets. Playing children were thrilled with such a find in those lean times, when nothing was available in stores, and when something was, it was so expensive that most could not afford it. In those early days, the Germans thought of many ways to decimate the Jewish population—germ warfare as well as concentration camps and murder.

The typhoid epidemic added to the town's misery, but it brought with it some benefits as well. The first was relief from the Germans. They disappeared, fearing the disease, and during the weeks of the epidemic, we slept relaxed. The town was quarantined, and we could leave our homes only during certain hours of the day. No one cared about the curfew or the quarantine, because we did not have to fear the Germans. The second benefit—I am not sure if it could be called that, although some people felt that it could—was an opportunity to be able to die a natural death in one's own bed.

The epidemic left our family untouched.

As soon as the quarantine was lifted, the Germans reappeared and at once conducted another akcja, this time during broad daylight, killing nearly a third of what was left of the townspeople, many of whom had just recently left their sick bed, having survived typhoid fever.

Twelve

This second akcja left a strong mental image with me because of one particular incident. Shayna's mother was shot and killed while peeling potatoes on the stoop of her home, and the eldest boy in that family was also killed during this second akcja. The father was left with seven fairly small children.

There was no need for the Germans to order Jews out of their homes this time because enough were on the streets—it was summer. Trucks full of Gestapo agents arrived at the market and dispersed in all directions, shooting at everyone they saw. Everyone became a target, even as they were running to hide. The panic and those terrible screams alerted us on Jagielonska Street to what was taking place.

When it all stopped and we dared show our faces at the kitchen window, the sight that met us defied description. It looked as if everyone in town had died a horrific death. The eerie stillness, the unmoving bodies, each lying in its own pool of blood—it looked as if the town were in a terrible sleep. People had fallen in their doorways, crossing streets; a mother with infant in her arms sat against a wall, their bullet-ridden bodies tightly enmeshed; an old bearded man lay on the road, blood pooling around him, his hands clenching prayer books to his chest.

Gripped by horror and desolation, my legs shaking, I gaped at the street then at Mother, whose contorted face reminded me of some caricature I had once seen in a museum. I thought about art, about Katowice, and about my friends here in Dabrowa, and I wanted everything to be normal, and I didn't want to look at the street anymore. I wanted to remove myself from this curse that hung over us, but I didn't know how to do it. I only knew that I wanted it and that I had to do something to escape this awful existence. I walked into the back room and opened a schoolbook to prepare my homework for the next day's lesson.

Later that day, some Germans came down our street, creating another panic, but they only walked through, looking over the horror that had been created earlier. Something must have struck them as funny because they laughed loudly and called to each other, pointing out things they found interesting. They were the only live people on the street; everyone else who had been outside had run for shelter when they'd heard them coming, and the soldiers' voices reverberated in the stillness.

Judging by their laughter, they found much to amuse them.

* * *

News from nearby towns and cities was all bad. Jews were being slaughtered everywhere. Some of the larger neighboring towns and cities had already become Judenfrei, a term that had come into daily use. Our town looked uninhabited. Houses where entire families had been killed stood empty. A window left open before its owners were shot continued to stay open. One had the impression of being in a ghost town.

Those of us still left living did not behave as we had before. People conversed in whispers, no longer congregating on the streets or anywhere else. The synagogue was locked and stood abandoned. People ran their errands furtively, stealing along the houses, afraid of being seen or stopped by anyone. Even old friends avoided each other. Most vendors sold their goods out of their homes, no longer setting up stands at the market. The atmosphere was one of deep mourning and mistrust.

School opened only sporadically. The student body was greatly diminished. I continued to attend, and there I saw my friends, but I no longer made visits to Alfred's house. I was allowed only to go to school or on important errands and never in the evenings. There was no guarantee that a shooting action would not take place during the day, but as long as school remained open, I attended, and I occasionally ran errands for Mother.

Weeks passed—terrible, scary weeks. Another akcja was expected, but everything continued to be quiet, so quiet, in fact, that it didn't seem real, and it caused more fear. The Germans were busy elsewhere. Suddenly, dozens of people began arriving in Dabrowa from other places, places that had become Judenfrei. New groups of refugees arrived daily, filling vacant houses. The town took on some of its old appearance. In a short time, Dabrowa was more crowded than it had ever been, with people out on the streets talking, shopping. Did the Germans plan it that way, thinning out the population in Dabrowa to make room for refugees from those Judenfrei towns? Maybe they wanted to crowd as many Jews as possible into one place to make it easier to dispose of greater numbers at once rather than having to ferret out small groups dispersed among Christians.

New merchants opened small stores; tailors, shoemakers took the place of those departed; and the cost of food kept rising as the demand for it grew. Food was available only through farmers who brought in their produce, hens, geese, eggs, and butter. Skimmed milk could be bought in the local government-run dairy. The one or two open grocery stores carried only flour, sometimes some sugar, and occasionally that dark, mysterious jam. Prices were not regulated, and merchants charged whatever they wanted, citing great difficulties in obtaining supplies. Since the town's population was captive because travel was forbidden, we were at the mercy of the merchants and of the farmers who brought in food, and we had to pay whatever was asked.

We now ate only when hungry. Mother made no regular meals. A slice of Mother's black bread and her ever-delicious potato soup was a fine meal.

It was good to have all these new arrivals because they made our town lively. I saw boys and girls in their teens all over and often heard their laughter. These new people were of a different class than those who had populated Dabrowa previously. They were urban, moneyed, worldly. They didn't skulk around as the rest of us did; they didn't seem as downtrodden. They seemed more sure of themselves despite their circumstances.

Now that the atmosphere in town was more cheerful, our group of friends was meeting again. Two new boys from Krakow came to our school, and they joined us. I will call the boys by their initials: D. was considered ugly because of a large nose and close-set eyes, and M., with his darkly handsome looks, soon had all the girls crazy about him. Not quite fifteen years old, M. would gladly have made love to every pretty girl in school—and he probably did to many. It looked as if he would have no trouble taking that monopoly away from Alfred. But although he possessed great looks, he did not have Alfred's knowledge of our countryside, and he could not swim, hike, or skate. Thus, whenever we planned an afternoon outing, M. would excuse himself, not wanting to appear less than the image his looks had created.

M. lived with his mother, a very young and strikingly beautiful woman, in a small apartment above a bakery on the edge of town. Soon his mother got mixed up with the baker—for bread, it was said.

D. came with both parents and several older sisters and brothers. They rented a house away from the center of town. They were a distinguished family of professionals. Always properly attired and impeccably mannered, they conducted themselves with dignity. One tended to excuse the absence of good looks in that family, even in our bourgeois circles, where great value was placed on appearance.

Another new arrival affected me and my family directly. He was a gentleman of about thirty. I do not remember his name, and I actually never knew his real name because he lived under various pseudonyms. When he first knocked on our door, it was afternoon, and I was doing homework. Mother opened the door to face what appeared to be a German in civilian clothing. He was dressed in tweeds, a leather briefcase under his arm. She looked at him speechless until he smiled and asked to be invited in. Taking him by the arm, she quickly pulled him inside the house.

They talked German, rapidly, using words with which I was not familiar. They laughed and seemed to enjoy their reunion. He was charming, tall, broad shouldered, with deep brown eyes, an olive complexion (or did he have a tan?), and longish light brown hair. When he laughed, he showed two rows of splendid teeth.

I sat watching them for a while, completely absorbed in themselves, but after the initial excitement passed, Mother looked around at me and introduced us. His response in German was, "She is very pretty," and "she will be lovely at eighteen." More laughter from both while I blushed and Mother's cheeks glowed the same way they did when my teachers gave her reports of my schoolwork.

When Father came home, there were whispered discussions until it was established that Mr. X would stay with us for a few weeks. He would sleep in the attic and spend most of the daylight hours there, coming down in the evenings for a walk and the evening meal.

At first he shared the attic with the chickens, sleeping on a mattress and using a featherbed for cover. He brought with him a very small collection of books and various papers, which occupied him during the day, I did not know to what purpose. Mr. X spoke several languages fluently. Although he seemed quite satisfied with his little office in the attic, I felt sorry for him. I could not tell why. Despite his charm and his good manners, he presented a sad countenance.

Mother cooked chicken dishes daily so that he might have the attic to himself. She said she would raise some again when our visitor left.

I was excited about this addition to our family. He brought an aura of mystery with him, and it was good to know that this exciting man lived above us, reading, walking about, working on his papers. Our evening meals were enlivened by his conversation, and I found myself looking forward to supper.

I raved to Mr. X during one of our suppers about how delicious Mother's potato soup was and that it could even be eaten cold. "In fact," I told him, "it tastes almost better when cold." He said that he would like to try it. So Mother prepared some and served it cold one evening. After tasting it, he admitted that it was, indeed, excellent, and inclining his head toward me said, "In France this is called vichyssoise." He was not French, but I assumed that he had been there, just as I assumed that he had been everywhere and that he knew everything. Because I was not allowed to ask him any questions, I made up my own stories about him, giving him the kind of interesting background a romantic figure like him deserved.

I was not allowed to talk to anyone about our guest. Only Grandmother, Aunt Franka, and Uncle Emil knew of this arrangement. Uncle Herman was not told because Mother was afraid he would inadvertently mention it to some of his young friends.

Sometimes Aunt Franka accompanied Mr. X on his evening walks, over Uncle Emil's objections. Mr. X used German identification papers, and away from our house, he "was" German. I wish I knew why he lived in this way. Certainly it could not have been for safety's sake. To save his life, he should not have been here where everyone knew that we were Jewish. Was he on some mission, spying? For whom? He could not have been spying during his stay with us because he was practically imprisoned in the attic, and nothing of any import happened during his exercise walks. At least we hoped that his walks were uneventful, for his sake. Was he a fugitive? My parents might have known, but I did not.

I have already mentioned that we had no radio and no telephone. Although there was a post office in Dabrowa, housed in a tall, red brick building of ancient vintage, I never saw any mail delivered to anyone during the war. Yes, Mr. X could gather certain information—for instance, he saw what was happening to Jews in this part of Poland, and he saw what kinds of relations existed between Jews and Christians—but how could he deliver this information to whomever he may have collected it for if he had no means of long-distance communication? I certainly do not see how he could have been able to gather any strategic information concerning the war. Yet, I overheard Mother and Father more than once talking in undertones about Mr. X's "work," and it had to do with spying. It would have been interesting to know why he lived as he did and why he hid out with us.

At first Mr. X was careful to follow Father's instructions. He left the attic at appointed times, careful to observe the routine laid out for him so that we too could be protected from implications. But after a while, he became reckless, no longer waiting for it to get dark before he went for walks, and even marching around town in broad daylight, often scaring people who didn't know who he was or what he was there for.

Once, while waiting my turn for skimmed milk in a long line at the dairy cooperative, I saw Mr. X approaching in long, firm strides, a forbidding look on his face. This must be his German look, I thought. Since I was told not to recognize him if ever I saw him on the street, I did not greet him, turning instead to face the back of the person in front of me. But he spotted me and stopped, then took me by the hand and led me straight to the front of the long queue, past all the people who were ahead of me, to where an old, retired school principal was portioning out the milk. Making his way forward with shouts in German, he told the old man to fill my pitcher at once. The man, his hands shaking, bowed and did as he was told while the rest of the people waiting in line, including me, gaped, stupefied. When my pitcher was full, he let me pay for the milk. Embarrassed, I thanked him in Polish and went home while he continued on to the outskirts.

As I walked home, I thought of what had just happened. He had seemed so completely German in looks, speech, and manner that it was easy for him to pass for a German. I was confused. I assumed that he was Jewish, but my parents and I never really discussed his nationality nor his religion. Could it be that he was a German soldier who had run away from the army and was hiding until he could go back home? I kept those thoughts to myself. I understood his reasons for wanting to walk during the days; he could see things better, and he could walk in the sun. On the other hand, he placed himself in terrible danger doing this. Once he started walking in daylight, Aunt Franka no longer accompanied him.

When I got home, I told Mother what had happened at the dairy. She was so shaken when she heard my tale that she resolved to talk to him as soon as he returned. She would remind him that he endangered not only his own life, but the lives of our entire family by acting in this reckless way. He might well imagine what the Germans would do to us were they to find out that we harbored a fugitive. The whole town might even be accused of complicity.

I knew that he always returned from his walks through back alleys so that he could enter our courtyard without being seen. That afternoon, I waited by the back room window until he returned. I saw him coming, furtively winding his way among the houses, afraid someone would spot him. How different he looks now, I thought. His large frame seemed to have shrunken. Father waited for him. "Irena," he said to Mother. "I will speak with Mr. X"—before she had a chance to do so. "I will tell him to stop his dangerous behavior before causing mass murder." She meekly answered, "Yes, Joske."

His stay with us did not last long. Someone betrayed him to the Germans. Several weeks after his arrival, two German policemen picked him off the street near the dairy. He did not resist. Meekly, without a word (where was his self-assurance, his skill with languages, his courage? Or did he lose the desire to save himself given the awful circumstances in which he lived?), he walked between the two policemen, passing our house, looking neither to the right nor to the left but straight ahead. Mother saw this as she sat at the kitchen window. Aunt Franka, sitting at her window across the street saw it too and lost no time following the three men at a safe distance. Mother was devastated. She ran across the street to Grandmother's and broke down in tears. She would not have been able to follow that procession.

Later Aunt Franka told us that they took him past the market, down toward the railroad station, and when they came to a grassy hill surrounded by trees, they told him to climb it. When he reached the top, he turned around and raised his arms in surrender. After only a single shot, he crumpled to the ground.

We didn't know what happened to his body. When Mother went by the spot the next day, it was not there. No one in our family went to claim his body because the Germans were watching and would murder anyone who did. To harbor someone like that man would have meant instant death, regardless of what his job was. It was enough that he had impersonated a German. Mother buried his briefcase in our courtyard and cleaned out his belongings from the attic. Working late at night to avoid being observed by neighbors, she tore his papers into shreds and burned all his notes in the kitchen stove, leaving his novels on a wooden shelf in the back room. Father would use his shirts and other clothing.

For days no one in our house spoke. We went about our chores and ate meals in silence. Aunt Franka's eyes did not dry for a long time. I missed Mr. X for his charm and good humor and for the diversion he had brought with him. But I didn't know who he was nor what mission he was on. He remains a sad mystery to this day.

Thirteen

Everyone knew we were due for an akcja. The Germans had not been as visible lately as they had been in the last two years. They were only around when confiscating property or carrying out shootings. Since the town had filled up with people from other cities, we reasoned that they would be planning to thin out the population again. And, indeed, following quickly one after another, we had two akcjas in two days. They arrived in open trucks, impeccably attired in pressed uniforms, gloved hands holding loaded pistols. At a shouted command, they dispersed over the town, well versed in what they were to do. And so from the darkness of an early dawn until the sun rose high above the houses, they hunted down their victims, stopping only to reload their pistols. When their quota was met, they gathered at the waiting trucks, their voices echoing against the despondent silence of the streets.

The mind boggles at how powerless we were. Why did we not fight back? By then we were so demoralized that it was easy to herd us to our death. Many were totally resigned to their fate. But mainly, I believe, we remained passive because we knew how futile it would be to fight the German army. Had there been those who would have been willing to fight back, they would have at best staged some disorganized resistance, poorly skilled as Jews were in combat in those days.

For hundreds of years, perhaps even thousands, Jews in Poland had been used to total submission to authority. I cannot imagine a Jewish rebellion at that time. Jews had not been allowed to possess weapons for a long time, and unless drafted and trained for army service, many would not have known how to use a gun. A community could not think of resistance unless it was ready for total and immediate annihilation. The smallest transgression of the law by one person brought on retaliation toward the whole community. The slightest attempt on a German would have brought on a swift and terrible response.

All of this made us easy targets. The now famous case of resistance in the Warsaw ghetto was a show of defiance. It could certainly not have been expected to produce a victory. It was a last desperate effort to die in combat rather than be slain at point blank range. It was a victory for the power of the human spirit, a noble attempt of a group of poorly armed, poorly trained young people against the might of the German army.

Feeling that the end was nearing, other Jewish communities in Poland that were still left at that time (1943, the time of the Warsaw ghetto uprising and Hitler's final solution, the total destruction of Jews and all things Jewish) also revolted, on a smaller scale. But all efforts in that direction were, of course, futile, and instead of helping to preserve life, they accelerated the arrival of death.

In Dabrowa, the Jewish community ceased to exist near the end of 1942. Until then, living as we did, isolated from the rest of the world through forbidden movement and the absence of newspapers or any communication with the outside world, we knew nothing of the eruptions of revolt, and when the war ended, I was amazed to learn of their existence.

People continue to be cruel to each other—that has not changed. But today any mistreatment of people in the remotest corners of the earth creates an outcry of the world community and usually receives immediate and, for a while, undivided attention. That has changed. Over the past several years, the world has responded to the plight of the Kurds, to Somalia, Rwanda, Haiti, Kuwait, Bosnia, the Palestinians. Would that a small measure of such care and such interest had been given to the people in countries occupied by the Germans in the Second World War.

When in 1942, at the height of the Nazi extermination programs, a few small boats carrying Jewish refugees were refused entry into Palestine by the British, who insisted on enforcing policies of the White Paper, limiting Jewish immigration to the country, no country objected sufficiently to stop this unreasonable British action. Returning to their country of origin, the refugees headed for death. And this was happening when the ovens at such mass-murder centers as Auschwitz, Birkenau, Treblinka, Sobibor, Lublin-Majdanek, Buchenwald, Chelmno, and many others were regularly fed gassed humans.   Some of the recent arrivals in Dabrowa left when things got too dangerous to remain there. They looked for other, bigger places, hoping they would not be found. But there were no safe places for Jews in Poland during the war. Villages were out of the question because they were so small that a single person who did not belong would immediately be recognized. They were also mostly inhabited by Christians, and a Jew would have had a hard time getting lost in the crowd. Large cities were Judenfrei, and it was not only difficult for a Jewish family to settle among Christians without being recognized, it was strange and difficult to live among people with whom one could not talk for fear of revealing one's religion. There was no place to go, and most of those who left were either taken off the road as they traveled or were shot when they were spotted leaving town.

We were by now so inured to murder that whether someone got killed or not was making little difference as long as that person was not a relative. It was the same as reading of terrorist attacks in today's newspapers. The mind gets used to gruesome things. Killings now took place at all hours of the day and night. Yet during the day, there still seemed to be some life in town. When night fell, an eerie stillness descended on the streets; no living sound could be heard, and no living being could be seen, not even an animal. Mechanically, we went about taking various precautions for safety: Father going up to the attic; Mother and I sleeping in our clothes.

Sleep was fitful as we waited for the harsh sounds of shots, of orders for us to come out of our homes—"Raus, alle Juden raus"— then shots and the screams of those who fell. What nights those were as we waited, exhausted from vigilance.

At the first sign of day, we removed our clothes, washed, and began the day. While never safe anymore, somehow the day brought with it relief. Sometimes after a rare, uninterrupted night of sleep, a new surge of energy would fill us with a zest for life. We spoke, told stories, ate with enjoyment. It was strange that we should so fear the night yet be so invigorated by the day when the akcjas no longer occurred only at night, and day was equally dangerous. In fact, the akcjas became more frequent during daylight, and instead of only shootings, hundreds were being taken away—no one knew where.

The Germans were more successful in rounding up their quotas during the day when people were running errands and going about their business. All they had to do was come to town and catch everyone on the streets. They rarely entered houses for fear of what might happen to them inside a house. Once they had enough people, they marched them down to the railroad station, where the captives were loaded on waiting freight cars and sent to unknown destinations. When these deportations began, the shootings diminished, and the akcjas became different: they started with soldiers surrounding the town so that no one would be able to leave. Then a few random people would be shot—the old, the slow-moving ill, and any visible child. Having thus thinned out the crowd, the rest would be rounded up and driven at a trot from every corner of town to the marketplace. Anyone unable to keep up the pace would be shot and left behind; the rest would be hurried on with shouts and the butts of rifles.

Groups were driven like cattle from back streets by no more than a few Germans screaming orders not to look around, to move quickly to join the rest in the market. Any deviation from what had been ordered met either with a bullet or the butt of a rifle.

This new kind of akcja lasted longer than the night akcjas. It usually took a whole day to gather all the groups hunted out of the many back streets and to drive them to the market. When the soldiers had their quota, they drove the assemblage down to the railroad station on foot, where the people were loaded into freight cars. So many were loaded in each car that they could only stand up, and fights broke out as competition heated up for a place near the tiny barred windows. Once the train left the station, all trace of these people was lost.

Because we had no connection with the outside world, nor even with neighboring towns, each place an island in a morass of bloody murder and terror that could be reached only on foot in the night, we had no idea that there were such places as Auschwitz or Treblinka. It was generally thought that those who were sent away were sent to work, but no one ever returned or was heard from, and the total secrecy that surrounded their whereabouts did not bode well. The fear from uncertainty that gripped us constantly intensified. Yet no one imagined the awful places these transports were going to. In time, a suspicion arose that perhaps these people were not taken to work but were being killed somewhere. Where? This became a constant topic of conversation, which was mostly based on guesswork and conjecture. Theories abounded, some of which proved later to be true.

People who lived along the route to the train and those who lived directly by the railroad told those of us who were left how these marches, or transports, proceeded once they left the marketplace. Christians were the only ones able to observe these proceedings, lining the streets and watching the railroad cars being loaded.

How the Germans distinguished between Jew and Christian by allowing Christians to observe is not known.

As people were marched to the railroad, some tried their luck by straying into a ditch or a clump of trees—if seen, they were shot on the spot. When the akcja was over, and people began to venture out of their homes, family members of those who had been taken walked along the transport route to look for their relatives, dead or alive.

Whenever a rumor of an impending akcja went around town, there would now be an exodus to the woods, of which the countryside was full. Most of the time, the rumors turned out to be false. Akcjas occurred when no one knew they were about to happen.

My parents always slept in town, depending on our attic in case of emergency, but I, encouraged by Father, started walking every night to the country. He felt that I had a good chance of saving myself there. To save one's life was all that mattered. No one gave any thought to what might happen to me if I were left alone, homeless, without money. The prevalent feeling was that all one ever needed was life, and everything else would follow naturally.

I didn't need to be told twice to go—the idea appealed to me at once. I knew the way well, and it was easy to walk the three or four kilometers each night and walk back in the morning. I enjoyed it. I always walked alone, and I was able to vary the trip by taking detours so that I could pass areas that I especially liked because of their physical beauty.

Most of the farmers in those nearby villages knew my father and his family, and they let me spend nights in their barns. They were well paid for this favor. Father took periodic trips to the country to leave money with each farmer who was willing to help so that in case we needed to hide, they would allow us to come.

Most were not helpful out of kindness, though some were better than others, showing compassion by not wanting to accept money. Basically, most did not like Jews and did not want any around, but "you are different," they told Father or me. That remark, which I heard so often in ensuing years from anti-Semitic friends, reminded me each time of the supposed flaws and shortcomings of those who shared my religion. I tried as hard as I could to figure out what those differences between us were, but I never came up with an answer.

In the country, I felt less afraid than in town, but I only felt free during the walk, because once I entered a barn, I had to stay there until the night passed, and I had to leave at first light. I was not allowed the freedom to walk around the farms.

I would leave home before it got dark, and as I left the town behind me, I could smell the clean, fragrant air. Each step lengthened the distance between me and the blood-stained streets, the frightened faces, the poverty, and the confinement. Here, everything was peace and beauty, and I gloried in it. I loved those trips alone, and I never felt lonely—there was so much to contemplate. I was able, during those trips, to achieve a measure of peace. I reflected on life and on nature during those precious solitary moments, a habit that stuck with me for life. Surrounded by fragrant hay, lying across the meadows in windrows, I could watch undisturbed the crimson sun sink into the horizon. Or I could walk between ripening cornfields, dotted with fiery poppies and deep blue cornflowers. I soon learned that there was not much point in picking them because they wilted in my hands even before I had picked a whole bouquet. I would then leave them by the side of the road, sad that I had torn them off their stems and deprived them of dying a natural death. Ruminating on things and observing nature, I might stop to look around me or slow my walk until it would suddenly be quite dark and I had to hurry not to lose my way and enter the wrong barn.

There were so many different, confusing paths in the country. All narrow trails, mere trampled grass some of them, it was easy to mistake one for another, and I needed to reach my destination by nightfall—exactly when night fell, not when it was still day, nor at dusk, but when it was dark enough for no one to see me entering the barn. I liked it when it was completely dark because I could then believe not only that I was the only person in the world, because I could not see anyone, but that I was also protected from harm by the darkness, because no one could see me.

Often the farmers whose barn I had slept in didn't even know that I had been there, because at the earliest light I rose, brushed the hay out of my hair, and smoothing down my clothes quietly let myself out of the barn to begin the walk back home. It was important not to let the farmer's neighbors see me because some might have denounced the farmer to the Germans. Punishment for harboring a Jewish child was severe.

As I neared town on those mornings, I would ask whomever I met how the night had passed. Most of the time it had been quiet, but not always. On the mornings when the news meeting me was good, I took my time walking back so that I could revel in nature's beauty, which never ceased to amaze and exalt me. On those good mornings, I knew that at home a breakfast would await me and a sponge bath and a change of clothes. Thus refreshed, in so many ways, I would take my books and go to classes, which miraculously continued for the few of us who still attended.

But on mornings when some passerby said, "Yes, there was one," I'd race home with a beating heart to find out if I still had parents or if that night had made me an orphan—the thing I had most feared as a child.

Today I see how miraculously my entire family kept surviving one akcja after another, and how I was spared the sight of even one family member's death. At the time, I did not think of this small blessing. I did not realize that I was lucky. Constant worry clouded my perspective.

Once, when I came home shortly after an akcja had taken place in the early morning hours, I met Mother leaving the house with a square of sugar between her teeth. I said good morning, and she answered but continued on her way, handing me the house key.

I asked about Father, and she said he is in town, but she was already across the street so that I could not question her anymore. I sensed, besides, that she would not talk, could not talk, that she wanted to be left alone. I understood that she felt like a stone, dead from continual fear, from the way we had to live: sleeping dressed, struggling for food, always afraid of being shot on sight. "Gehenna," Mother called it.

I watched her walk toward the market in her summer coat, which hung loosely about her gaunt frame, a gray wisp of hair tied at the nape of her neck. "Oh Mother," I moaned when I entered the house and threw myself on her bed, loud sobs shaking all of me.

A few days later, on my way home from school, a panic arose on the street, and I suddenly found myself being swept along with other people to a strange attic. I looked around at the silent faces, fear written all over them, but I was not able to contemplate that for long because my attention was diverted by masses of fleas attacking my bare legs. The futile attempts to rid myself of these biting insects kept me busy until a child came up to tell us that it was all right to come down.

Only one or two people were shot that day. The story told later was that a famous killer named von Malutki had arrived in Dabrowa and, to satisfy his urge to kill, had taken a walk into town and randomly shot at two men standing on the street talking. He had then turned around and walked back to German headquarters.

When I got home that afternoon, I found Mother preparing supper and Father splitting wood for the kitchen stove. Momentarily, a thankfulness arose in me, and all my love went out to God for being so blessed as to have a clean place to live, where I never saw nor felt an insect.

Whenever I was happy about something or felt grateful for something, I always thanked God. Even in the woods, gathering mushrooms or berries and enjoying the beauty of nature, I expressed my gratitude to God. Sleeping soundly in a barn full of hay, it did not occur to me to thank Father for paying off the farmer so that I would be allowed to stay there. Instead, I thanked God. So now, too, I thanked God for giving me a clean house to live in, never for a moment thinking that it was Mother who was responsible for my care and the cleanliness of my existence and not God, who was far away and quite possibly did not care if I was provided for or not.

The killings and the deportations so thinned out the population that the town again took on the look of a ghost town, and its eeriness again changed people's behavior to what it had been before the influx of refugees. Except for a person here or there, hurrying on an errand, the streets stood empty. People in Dabrowa never congregated again.

Uncle Emil stopped paying his daily visits to the confectionary to talk with other men. And that establishment was soon closed anyway. Father spent his time with Mother and me at home. I was not allowed to go to Alfred's to meet friends because seizures of people in broad daylight occurred with such frequency that no time of day or night was safe, and no one could predict when, suddenly, there would be an akcja. Fewer than two thousand Jews remained in town.

A young woman living on our street and her fiancé, who was spending the night in her house, were frightened out of their beds when an akcja occurred. When the lovers ran out of the house to cross the street, a shot hit her in the neck, blowing off her head.

Later that day, I saw the blond, bobbed head lying face down in the gutter.

Vovek's brother, Moniek, was also shot that night as he was coming home after a night out with friends. Hearing shots, he had turned in the opposite direction and started running away from town. A German pursued him and shot him just as he climbed a fence. His body remained hanging on the fence until his mother, Rachel, Mother's friend, found him the next morning.

By now Rolla's house stood empty. Stella and her mother were no longer with us, and the grain merchant, with his big beautiful house, his wife, and his youngest son, with whom I had sometimes played when I had first arrived in Dabrowa, were shot in their beds one night while sleeping. Eva, the grain merchant's daughter, and Uncle Herman no longer hid their close friendship—they were nearly always together. I don't know what happened to Eva's husband and baby.

On a certain afternoon, I was in Grandmother's house sitting on the window seat, doing algebra because the tables at home were being used by Mother for a sewing project. I happened to glance up from my book to see the one or two people who had ventured out running into their homes. Since I was at home, I continued to work, not giving this much thought. I was conditioned to panic, danger, death—all of these things were a part of my life.

In back of me sat Father, Uncle Emil, and Uncle Herman, talking. Grandmother and Aunt Franka were across the street helping Mother with her sewing. Suddenly there was a loud banging on the entrance to the house, and the door flung open with a crash.

Father and my two uncles immediately ran up to the attic, where, amid old furniture and various other discards, a shelter had recently been built. I tried to follow them, but it was too late. Two men had already entered the hall and saw me trying to run up the dark stairway behind Uncle Herman.

One of these men was Arthur, a Polish man in his early twenties whom I knew by sight. The other one was in German uniform, a loaded pistol in his hand. They both spoke Polish. We later found out that the man in uniform was a Folksdeutche, the first in a number of steps to becoming a full German (actually a member of the German ethnic group, but in those days that word identified a person who applied and was eligible for German citizenship). Having been given a German uniform, he was exercising his newfound power. They spotted me and looked as if they would follow me up the stairs, but I stopped, as did Uncle Herman. Father and Uncle Emil were invisible. Some muffled movement was heard in the attic, and the uniformed man ran up to look around, bumping into things because it was totally dark there. His friend, Arthur, did not like this. He called to him with some urgency to come down. They are afraid, I thought as I watched the soldier nimbly run down the stairs past Uncle Herman and me in response to Arthur's call.

There were two other men in the hall: the egg merchant, packing eggs, and his customer, the father of the seven orphaned children who lived a few houses away, the man whose oldest daughter, Shayna, wife, and oldest son had already been murdered. Both men stood petrified, watching, waiting.

When the uniformed man came down from the attic, he pushed the father of seven out the back door with the barrel of his gun, into the courtyard, and shot him twice. Not a word was spoken between murderer and victim. Coming back, the soldier wordlessly pointed his gun in the direction of the egg merchant, beckoning him to walk toward him, which the merchant did. The soldier shot him at point blank range right in the hall. I looked on, horrified at his corpulent, black-clad body on the floor, blood oozing out of his chest, grotesquely running down to his neck, where his beard dammed its flow.

I was too numb to utter a word, but presently a long mournful wail tore out of my chest—it was a sound I had never heard myself make before, or since. Arthur gave me a dirty look but did not say anything. Up to that point, he had ignored me. Now that I began to cry, he glanced at me. Encouraged, I started begging for my life. I directed myself exclusively to him, but he turned away.

The soldier meanwhile looked up the stairs at my young uncle standing behind me and motioned him to come down.

The situation had by now changed somewhat. The soldier did not seem as crisp as he had been when they had first stormed into the house. He was also reloading his revolver while slowly leading the way out to the backyard, meaning for Uncle Herman to follow him. But instead of following, Uncle jumped off the last few steps, turned to the front door, and with lightning speed disappeared. The soldier, realizing what was happening, followed in a fury. He was gone a long time—long enough for me to know that this was my chance. I begged and implored. An invisible force, a tremendous energy, kept pushing me to beg for my life. I continued without let-up, looking at Arthur, my tear-stained face contorted in pain and fear. I knew that when the soldier returned, it would be my turn. I didn't have much time.

It makes no difference what I said. I could not possibly remember each word—perhaps I do not want to remember— but the words were desperate, I know, incoherent, repetitious, interrupted only by long convulsive sobs. "Are you not afraid?" was a phrase I kept repeating feverishly, as if I were judging him. And not once did he look up at me or utter a word. Is he going to let me live? I wondered. It was difficult to tell. He did not move; he did not speak.

When the soldier's footsteps were heard on the pavement outside, Arthur gave me a long look and turned to meet his friend at the door. Speaking German now he said, "Das Fräulein lassen win." As if he had expected it, the soldier did not even look in my direction, and they both left.

Minutes passed, and I continued to cry. I could not stop. I tried moving my legs; they were stiff. Taking one step at a time, I moved down the stairs, planting both feet securely on each stair. Every move caused pain. It felt like learning to walk after an illness, and I realized then that I had been standing rooted to my spot during the entire episode. About halfway down, I saw through the open back door the soles of a pair of shoes and legs in trousers tightly twisted together. Another step, and I saw the upper body of the father of seven; another step, and there was the head, eyes wide open, looking up to heaven.

I jumped the rest of the stairs and ran to the front door but halted there. The street was a graveyard. Doors and windows of each house were tightly shut. I looked around. No one. I turned back into the hall and sat down on an empty egg crate—one corpse lying at the end of the hall, the other out in the backyard. I wailed, a resigned mourning wail, an acceptance of what had happened, not a desperate cry nor a fearful one, a piteous lament. I cried because I felt terribly alone, and even then I realized, though I could not have put it into words, that I would always be alone, because that ultimately is the human condition. Aloneness.

Each time I looked at the body of the egg merchant at the end of the hall, I wondered about his wife and daughter. Where were they? Did they know what had happened to him? "Dear God, where are you?" I repeated over and over.

Careful not to step on the bleeding body, I went out to the courtyard, where I thought I heard a moan. I looked down and waited for another sound. Then I realized that it was not the man in the yard whose moan I had heard, but the egg merchant in the hall. I turned to look at him and detected a very slight movement in his arm. Seeing that, I began pounding desperately on the door of his apartment, calling his wife and daughter, who, I thought, were shut in their bedroom. They both came out dazed.

I told them what I had seen and heard. They ran to him, crying hysterically, the wife falling on her husband and asking what she should do to help, but he only pointed to his pocket, where he apparently had some money. She took the money, sending her daughter to get a doctor. When the girl returned, she was alone. The doctor to whose home she had run through back streets did not want to risk his life by coming out of hiding. (By now the town knew that something terrible was happening in my Grandmother's house.) Helpless and incapable of doing anything else, the egg merchant's wife continued to scream and to rend her clothes. Finally the man gave a barely audible moan, saying, "Go in, I'm dying . . ." And both women went into their apartment, shutting the door. Today it seems incredible that they would leave him to die by turning away to the safety of their home.

I remained in the hall, not entirely alone. Keeping me company was the dying man, and just outside the hall lay the corpse. Upstairs in the shelter were my father and Uncle Emil.

The front door stood open to the street, which was devoid of life. I sat down in the groove on the front step—the only visible human being on the street. After a moment, I went back inside and sat again on the egg crate. I cannot tell why I didn't run across the street to my house, nor can I understand why Mother, Grandmother, or Aunt Franka did not come to get me. I can only reason that everyone was catatonic, just as I was, too dazed to know what to do but wait, not really knowing what for.

Suddenly I heard steps on the sidewalk, and I looked out to see a German policeman heading in my direction. As he reached the house, he looked down at me—a long look—then at the dead man in the backyard and the moaning man in the hall. I watched him ready his pistol, and I went out front to sit on the stoop again, oblivious of the danger I was in. Then I heard the shot, and the moans ceased. As he was leaving, the policeman lifted my weeping face by the chin, looked for a moment, then left without a word. I do not know why I was spared.

As soon as his steps died down, hysterical screams came from across the street. That brought me to reality. I instantly jumped off the stoop and raced across, where the door to my house had opened as the three women, Mother, Aunt Franka, and Grandmother, were coming out of the house. Brushing past them, I ran in the house for shelter, and they followed me back in, each in her turn throwing her arms around me with exclamations, hugs, and tears.

Mother spent that evening sitting at the kitchen window without speaking. She was still there in the morning when I asked her to make breakfast. Father remained in the shelter across the street, and Aunt Franka and Grandmother stayed locked up in their apartment while the two men who had been shot were being buried.

When Father came home from the shelter, he told us that he and Uncle Emil knew that I was alive because they not only heard everything and followed each detail while they were concealed in their spot, but they were able to watch some of what was going on through cracks in the wood of the shelter.

Uncle Herman was found in a friend's house on the outskirts of town, unharmed. He remained there for several days, fearing his pursuer would return to look for him out of anger for not having caught him the first time.

After that incident, I was greeted with special warmth wherever I went, and because so many people talked about it, the story got bigger, and it changed so many times that some versions even had me dead. People were surprised to see me, and they wanted every detail from the "horse's mouth." I did not want to talk about it.

Days later Grandmother told me how she and Aunt Franka had seen the egg merchant selling eggs to the father of seven in the hall before they crossed the street to help Mother with her sewing. She said that they had counted the shots they heard, and they were certain that I was alive because they knew that the killer would go after the men before he picked me. They also hoped that Father and Uncle Emil were in the shelter, and since they had heard only the two shots, they figured that they were, thinking that the egg merchant and the father of seven were the first to have been shot. Standing against the wall by the kitchen window, they were able to watch, unobserved, some of what was going on across the street. They saw Uncle Herman gain considerable distance when he bolted out of the house, before the soldier followed him. They became hysterical only when they later saw a German arriving and heard the third shot. They thought that now my turn had come—then they saw me sitting on the stoop, the German walking away.

I guess there is a whole story behind that third shot, but I am not sure I know what that story is. How did the Germans know that one of the men was still alive, causing them to send another to finish him off? Days later, rumor had it that the doctor to whom the egg merchant's daughter had run for help had informed the Germans that the job was incomplete. That was the rumor, but was it true? Who knows. After the war, I met some people from Dabrowa who had survived concentration camps, and they said that that same doctor collaborated with the Germans in the camps on various experiments using Jewish inmates as guinea pigs. The doctor was a Jew.

Today, nearly seventy years after that incident, I find it difficult to understand, even having lived through it, how one man with a gun could so terrify an entire town of people that they did not show the slightest resistance to what was being done to them, that they allowed themselves to be slaughtered without protest.

Fourteen

I virtually grew up in America, having come here in my formative years, and I am used to hearing people speak their minds and claim their rights, even resisting authority to achieve what is their right, and today I cannot understand blind submissiveness. But in the days when Germans occupied Poland, there were no such things as human rights, and Jews were not only despised by the Germans but had for hundreds of years been forbidden many freedoms by the Polish government and other governments in nearby countries. Living for generations under restrictions had made Jews humbly obedient, unresisting, submissive.

I remember how frightened we all were, frightened especially of losing our lives. Fear changed many people, leading them to commit deeds they never would have considered before. Fear for one's life—the worst of all fears—can render one lethargic and insensitive to everyone and everything except self-preservation. There were few heroes at that time. Remaining alive was the uppermost thought on everyone's mind. I never knew of any talk or plan for staging a front of resistance in Dabrowa. Perhaps if there had been access to weapons, or perhaps if news from other places could have reached us that some were planning to fight back, or perhaps if some encouragement could have reached us from our allies who fought in that war, we might not have felt as abandoned and might have had more courage to resist. But isolated as we were—vulnerable and helpless—each of us ran to his hole to hide. Resistance meant certain death; hiding out still left hope of possible survival.

It was at this time that all classes were canceled and school was closed. The Germans forbade group gatherings, but even if they hadn't, no one felt safe enough to attend. Many students had lost their lives, many families were torn apart, and a regular class would not have been possible anymore. Classes were never resumed. Thus ended my elementary education.

Life became even more hellish, if that's possible, than it had been until then. We were rarely left in peace for more than a week at a time. Violent death was something we expected daily. We lived in a constant state of mourning. Men, women, and children were picked off the streets and out of their homes for deportations to the unknown. No businesses remained, not the bakery nor the cobbler shop. Nothing, nothing. City after city, town after town, became Judenfrei, and Dabrowa received another small shipment of people, this time from Tarnów because that city had become Judenfrei too. Our landlady, who had been living with her son there, did not come back to Dabrowa, nor did her son. We didn't know what had happened to them.

Many of the houses belonging to people who had been killed or sent away were made off limits. No one knew what plans the Germans had for these homes, which stood unoccupied, showing messy interiors, left in haste. With many houses not available for occupancy, there was a shortage of housing for some of the new arrivals. My parents took in a family of two boys and a father. The conditions under which we now lived were deplorable. Mother was so deeply unhappy, and I suffered watching her. She loved order and cleanliness, but that was impossible to achieve in our small house now occupied by four men and two women. Yet, she would not have it any other way. These new arrivals were homeless, and like other families, my parents felt it incumbent upon them to offer help.

Mother was constantly busy doing something, and she never sat at the kitchen window anymore to rest after her daily chores. She didn't seem to mind the discomfort, but she minded the mess. She was the only woman waiting on four men. I tried to help, but she did not let me do much, admonishing me instead to study. I could not understand why I needed to study if I was going to die anyway.

The two boys who stayed with us were in their mid-teens. They had lost their mother during an akcja, and every night before going to sleep, they spoke for hours about her, often crying bitterly and without restraint. To listen to them affected us so that since their arrival, none of us had gotten any rest. Then my parents began to accompany me to the country for the night. The reasons were twofold: to get some sleep and to escape, at least for a few hours, our difficult situation at home. Those nights we slept mostly in the woods, hidden by dense brush or behind some tree, huddling together to keep warm and to shield each other from the dampness of the night. It was so good to be able to sleep through the night and to wake to the quiet, fragrant surroundings at the break of day. On the way back to town, we walked separately, each taking a different path so as not to create an obvious picture. Being discovered by a hostile farmer or by the Germans meant instant death or a trip to the unknown.

After one such night in the country, we came back to an empty house. There had been an akcja, and the father with his two sons had been taken. There was no blood anywhere in the house, and so no evidence of them having been shot. When people were being taken away to be deported, a little hope remained that some day they would return. No one imagined the horrific camps these people were being sent to. No one imagined the gas chambers and the ovens that operated constantly, killing as many as possible in the least amount of time, at the least expense—wholesale murder.

There were no longer any discussions about where those who had been taken away might be because people did not get together to talk, and at home, talk was minimal. No one really knew anyway. There was hope that they were alive, and because of that hope, it was preferable to be sent away than to be shot on the spot. People became so used to losses, to indignities, to brutalities that we became like animals who are constantly being abused by their owners but who stay around anyway because they have no place to go.

Fifteen

It was spring 1942, and we were going to the country together almost nightly. I went every night, and my parents went most nights with me. Sleeping in the woods was easy. Also, because Father had made arrangements with some farmers to allow us to sleep in their barns occasionally, we didn't sleep outdoors in inclement weather all the time.

It was spring, and it rained a lot. The three of us were planning to spend the night in a farmer's barn. This night a "final" akcja was expected, leaving Dabrowa Judenfrei. Rumors were often wrong, but because they were sometimes right, we could not take the chance of ignoring them. We left home early in the evening, and when we reached the farmer's barn where we were to spend the night, it was pitch dark. The farmer's house had a fence around it, and the gate was locked. Father did not want to wake him, so we jumped the fence and into a bed of rosebushes. I could not suppress a low moan because of the scratches on my legs, and that brought the farmer out of the house.

"Who is it?" he roared.

"It's Josef," answered Father, quietly going toward him. "We need to spend the night in the barn. They say it will be a bad night in town."

"Yes, so I've heard, and that's why I want to have no Jews on my property tonight. What if they come all the way out here looking for some?" He faced Father, who remained silent, stunned for a few seconds, thinking of what to say to change his mind. But the farmer would not budge. He demanded we leave at once.

"You'd better be going," he said with finality. "I want to go back to bed. Oh yes, and don't stay in my fields either." He walked to the gate, unlocked it, and lifted the latch to let us out.

"What about the money I gave you? Wasn't that for just such a night?" Father persisted, but the farmer waved him away. "There'll be other nights. Tonight, I don't want you here." We walked away.

The night was chilly, and the ground, heavy with water from recent rain, squished under our feet. After two or three kilometers, we sat down in the wet grass, exhausted. We knew that we were not safe sitting in the open like this. If any of the farm workers saw us, they would know immediately who we were and why we were there. Some would let us be, but some would go to the Germans, who would come back with them to take us away.

We were not sure where we were in this total darkness, but because we needed a rest and did not know where else to go, we simply dropped on what seemed like a path between two fields of young corn. We sat close together, leaning on each other, Mother's coat hung over our heads as an umbrella. I peered into the darkness, wondering at the mystery of it all, my fertile mind giving way to dreams despite the discomfort and the fear.

We heard no distant shots, saw no light, heard no barking dogs. I fell asleep. When I woke up, my parents were stretching their legs nearby. In the east the sky was red with the rising sun, and at the opposite end, a crescent moon was fading away.

Starting off slowly, we began the trek back home. As the sun rose higher and took the chill out of our bodies, the grass began to dry, making our walk easier. We picked up speed, and the distance back didn't seem as long as it had seemed the night before.

Nearing town, we met some traders out on the road, waiting for farmers who brought in food for them to buy and resell. When we asked them about the night, they told us that it had passed quietly. We had lost a night. We could have stayed in our beds.

Upon our return, Father went straight to market to see what food he might be able to find while Mother and I went home to wash and change. After that night, Father decided to build a shelter in our back room. He said that at least that way we might save ourselves exhaustion, possibly even illness, not to mention the wrath of some farmer. He also thought that we might be safer in our own home if we could hide in it than we would be exposed in a field or in a barn where we were not wanted.

The spot he chose for this project was under the brown trunk that held our food provisions. There the wooden floor planks were wide and loose; they moved up and down when stepped on. Father felt that there was probably nothing more than earth underneath, which would be easy to scoop out, providing as much space as we needed.

Fired up and excited at the prospect of being able to outwit the Germans, he went to work, with Uncle Emil as helper. At first they floundered a little because this was not the same type of shelter they had built together in Grandmother's attic, where all they had done was make a narrow corridor along an existing wall by building a fake wall alongside it. Father's shelter was more complicated; it required cutting open the wooden floor and scooping out what was underneath it. They eventually accomplished this by cutting two lengths of the oak planks large enough for a person to pass through. They then dug deeply into the earth under the house, filling buckets and emptying them out the back window, into the courtyard.

It took several days to dig a hole big enough for three people to stand in. Once inside, Father would reach out and move the trunk back into position, then he would replace the cut planks from inside the shelter. Whoever entered the room would find nothing out of place. Even if the trunk were moved, the floor would look undisturbed—that is how well the planks fit back into place. It would have been nearly impossible for a stranger to tell that there was an opening.

But surrounded on all sides by earth, the air in the shelter was musty, and there was little of it. That was a serious drawback. There was no way to ventilate the area, and we could not possibly have remained there longer than perhaps half an hour without suffocating. Nonetheless, when it was finished, Father was proud of his shelter, and we were all relieved to have an alternative to those country trips and to our attic, which no longer seemed safe because the Germans were becoming aware of people hiding in attics.

We never used our new shelter, perhaps because we knew that we could not survive in this narrow, airless quarter, or perhaps because we never had a chance to use it.

June was unusually hot. Father made arrangements with a friendly farmer for a couple of weeks in his barn. This was not meant to be a vacation; rather, we were trying to get away from town, where daily rumors of a final catastrophe were now so unremitting that they began to sound real. "Dabrowa will become Judenfrei this month" was a sentence on everyone's lips, and it sounded like a death knell. Even without being able to gather in one place, people communicated, and everyone spoke of the anticipated disaster.

Maybe because it was so hot, or maybe because she was tired of running, Mother was listless, and preparations for our leave were going slowly. The house was too warm for comfort, and none of us spoke very much. We moved like robots. Finally, our day of departure came, and as soon as the sun set, we took, each of us, a bundle of clothing and other valuables to serve as insurance for food (the barn was paid for in advance) and set out on foot for the village where we were to spend the next two weeks.

As we got farther away from town and its oppressive atmosphere, we began gradually to feel more invigorated, enjoying the silence of our surroundings whenever we paused for a rest.

Leaving the main road by which we traveled, we took a sharp right turn onto a path that led to the farm where we were to stay. When we reached the whitewashed hut, it was completely dark, and feeling safe from being seen by anyone, Father knocked on the door while Mother and I waited behind. The farmer gave Father some instructions, and the three of us went across the yard to the barn.

This structure was about three stories high. On the right of the entrance, bales of hay were stacked almost to the roof. That was where the farmer wanted us to stay, on the very top so that when his help came in the morning, they would know nothing about us because they would not see us.

We climbed up, taking our bundles with us, and inhaling the sweet fragrance of hay. Once on top, my parents spread blankets and the small pillows we brought along, and we sank luxuriously into our hay shelter. In this manner, we were to spend two weeks, walking out in the evenings only to stretch and get exercise and to take care of bodily needs. We were not allowed to talk above a whisper, and that only when no one was around. The farmer made this an absolute condition of the arrangement, and Father agreed without question. Not only did the farmer not want anyone to know that he was hiding Jews, but had anyone discovered our being there, they might have given us away. So it was to our advantage as well as to his to follow the farmer's rules.

The village in which we were hiding was merely a scattering of a few wooden huts, each situated inside a few acres of land that belonged to it, and one or two larger farms. We were in the barn of one of those larger farms. This village, like most others surrounding Dabrowa, had no school, no post office, nor any other official building. If there was a church, it must have been far away because we never heard its bells.

I clearly remember the first night in the barn. We lay in the hay, looking at the sky and the flickering stars through crevices in the boards. Sleep came quickly, and it was a deep, peace-restoring sleep that lasted late into the morning, when the farmer's wife came up with our first meal of the day.

Twice each day, in the mornings, after all the help was out in the fields, and evenings, when they had left to go home, the farmer's wife brought food, which usually consisted of potatoes, sour milk, dumplings, and cabbage. Here I ate for the first time hot millet with milk as a first meal of the day, and I learned to like it. I would not have touched this at home. I have not eaten millet since the war, but I still remember its pleasant taste. Our hunger was great, and it would have been difficult to say if the food was well prepared or not. To us it was heavenly.

We got lots of rest, especially at night, when we could sleep undisturbed and without worry of being dragged out of bed or of being shot. We did not talk much. We weren't allowed to. We simply lay in the hay during the day, taking our walks at night, where a special private path was recommended by the farmer for safety. This path circled his cherry orchard, and even though we could not see much when the nights were dark, we always stopped for a few moments to look at the rows of trees. I longed to come here in daytime when the sun shone. I wanted also to go in the courtyard, where chickens ran freely, and to the stables to look at the cows and horses. But we were shut out of normal life and had to be satisfied with stalking around at night and hope no one would discover us.

I felt desperately sad during those nocturnal walks because I felt odd having to hide like this. I wanted to be like other people. I wanted my life to be normal. I wanted to live in the country with the farmer and his family in the open. I hoped God would know my thoughts.

As our stay was nearing its end, Mother and I finished the books we had brought with us, and Father was tired of looking at his business accounts from Katowice. For two weeks we had been isolated from the awful reality that was our present life, and for these two weeks, we got a small taste of what it might be like to live once again without fear, even with limited freedom. During our last evening in the barn, Mother made a few simple preparations for our trip back, and it was decided that I would go ahead, to see if it was possible for us to return. And so, early the next morning, long before sunrise, I left the farm, wearing several layers of clothing (wearing more meant having to carry less), one on top of the other, topped by a light overcoat, leather shoes, stockings, and a scarf on my head. In my hand I carried a small bundle of odds and ends: Father's woolen socks, some underwear, a sweater. Mother fully believed that we were returning home, which was why she let me take some of our things back.

I made my way across the fields. It was still cool and quiet. An occasional barking dog could be heard in the distance while I walked along briskly, thinking of home. From time to time, I turned to see how far I had gone, and when I could no longer see the farm, I knew I had covered half the distance to Dabrowa.

Dawn was creeping in slowly, and before me stretched a green meadow. The soft grass looked inviting, but I could not waste time lying in it for a rest because I was on a schedule. I decided to run for a while so that I could lie down later for a few minutes, after which I would again run for a distance, and so on.

Before I left the farm, my parents had cautioned me to follow my schedule because it would offer the greatest safety. I was to reach Dabrowa at a certain time of morning, and I was to return to the farm by nightfall. I was sent to find out what the conditions were in town and if it was safe for us to return. I was told not to linger. Our two weeks at the farm were up. The farmer wanted us to leave.

Thinking back, this trip seems like a tall order for a twelve-year-old girl, wearing layers of warm clothing on a summer day, having to be alert to mortal danger, and having to walk several kilometers each way on a tight schedule. But I was sent ahead because with my so-called Aryan looks, my parents thought I would be safe, a whole lot safer than a group of three on foot, in heavy city clothes, carrying bundles.

It was a time when we were playing with our lives. We were the hunted, the unarmed, the fully vulnerable against the hordes of cruel hunters who by now outnumbered us, and if it was safer for me to go ahead to reconnoiter the area than it might have been for my parents to do this, then I was without hesitation ready to do it. I followed the plan they made—it would not have occurred to me to question the wisdom of it—and I was not afraid. I was actually glad to be given the responsibility.

Playing the game of running and resting, I worked my way through the meadow, and as I reached the small hill that separated it from the path on which I was to continue, the sun rose out of the earth, and I stopped resting. I had to reach town before anyone could see me, and not until the sun rose did I realize that I was losing time. I suddenly became fully aware of the insecurity of my position.

Standing on the crest of the hill, I noticed a few figures moving in my approximate direction. I quickly looked around for a hiding place, but save for a few shrubs and young trees, there was only the dusty, well-worn path leading to town. It would have been pointless to hide anyway because I had already been noticed. They were heading directly toward me. I could see that it was a group of boys calling out various unmentionable greetings. They were ruffians with disheveled hair; some had scarred faces.

"Where are you going?" asked the biggest, a broad unpleasant grin on his face.

"To town," I answered off-handedly, hiding my fear.

"Well, you certainly have courage." He was still grinning rudely and looking at his friends. "Don't you know that all Jews have been killed? Aren't you afraid to go there?"

"Oh, but I'm not Jewish," I ventured in the same tone as before.

"Stop lying, you damn Jew." He got serious, angry. "And how come you're so fat? I thought Jews in hiding didn't get much to eat." I kept silent, the skin on my back curling.

"You know what I think," he continued to taunt. "I think you're wearing more than one dress under that coat. I have a little sister. She may be able to use some of your clothes. She never had any such things as you are wearing." He gave a short laugh, then turned to his friends. "Boys, help the young lady take off her clothes." He laughed more, showing decayed teeth. When he uttered the words "young lady," he bowed mockingly, and a wisp of dank hair fell over his eyes. He let it hang there while he watched two of the boys rip the coat off me and then one dress. They told me to sit down so they could take off my shoes and stockings. They also took the scarf off my head, all the while obeying orders from their leader. Then they stopped.

Moving away a few paces from me to get a better look, the leader looked me up and down and finally said, "You're much thinner now," and muttering something under his breath that caused the others to laugh raucously, he picked up the clothes and threw them over his shoulder. "Now let's see what's in the bundle," he said. Fingering the soft wool of the socks, he exclaimed, "Oh, nice wool socks, underwear. My mother will be glad to get these things." My clothes over his shoulder, the bundle in his hand, they moved on. "God be with you [szczesc Boze]," he called out. They left me standing barefoot, stunned. In a daze, I kept looking at my coat and dress hanging from his shoulder as I watched them go.

I fought not to let tears get the best of me. Swallowing hard, I reminded myself that I was very lucky to still be alive. The boys disappeared out of sight, and I turned my face to Dabrowa as I started again, a soothing dew bathing my feet.

The sun was getting warmer, and I reasoned that it was actually good not to have so many pieces of clothing on me. Had the boys not done it, I would have had to take off and carry some of it.

As I reached the outskirts of town, I passed that person's house where not too long ago Uncle Herman had hidden. Then I passed the bakery, above which M. and his mother had lived. I saw no movement anywhere, but I attributed this to the early hours. I quickened my step. I wanted to be among those whom I knew and where I felt less vulnerable. I wanted to be with Grandmother, with friends. I wanted to see familiar faces, and I rushed ahead. But the eerie silence frightened me, and I remembered that no one ever slept late in Dabrowa. The town was usually up with the dawn. I began to think about what the hoodlums had said: "Don't you know that all Jews have been killed?" When I finally reached the sidewalk that led to Jagielonska Street, our street, I became unsure of my safety, and I decided to continue through the back alleys into Grandmother's courtyard.

There was no one anywhere. I looked into Mindy's empty apartment, the blue-painted wall of her large workroom with its rows of wigs hanging in order, from very dark to light blond. Nothing was moved. There was no sound of any kind. It was as if I were the only person alive. Doors, windows, stood wide open. I could have wandered in and out of any of the houses undisturbed. Some of the doors were torn off their hinges; the ground was strewn with broken glass where windowpanes had been pushed in.

I looked in some of the houses and saw plates with unfinished food standing on tables, beds in disarray, clothing lying around on the floors. In this confusion, I glimpsed parts of human bodies; arms, heads—their brains spilled out, grotesque expressions on their faces—ears, all blood stained. And everywhere a menacing silence. Nothing stirred, not even a cat or a dog. A town petrified. I stopped looking into houses. I moved faster. A desperate feeling of being trapped enveloped me—it felt as if the whole town was a cage, holding me in its grip and giving me no avenue of escape.

I moved noiselessly, afraid of making a sound, confused thoughts racing through my head. "What shall I do? Go back to the country or continue on to our house? There must be someone around who could tell me what the situation is for those who are left alive."

I wanted an explanation of what was actually quite clear. Hadn't those boys told me what had happened? I refused to accept this, so I plodded along, careful not to step on anything with my bare feet, until I came to the narrow passage between houses that led back to Jagielonska, at the end of which I could see my house across the street. I went straight down through the passage and peeped out, looking up and down the street. No one. Dear God, I thought, help me.

Should I cross the street to my house and be completely exposed— one living human being on a deserted street, a perfect target—or should I turn around and head back to the country? Holding on to the large house key, I began to whimper. From across the street, I looked at our gray-painted door, the three crooked steps in front of it, and the kitchen window with its lace curtain neatly in place.

For the first time since pleading with Arthur for my life, I felt utterly endangered. (I had not felt the same danger when earlier that day the boys were taking my clothes from me.) For the first time since that day a few months ago, I felt what it was like to be terrified out of reason—all resources left me, and I did not know which way to turn. I stood there waiting for the moment of confusion to pass, and when my thoughts momentarily cleared, I realized that I was alone in a deserted town in which all life seemed to have been extinguished. What was I doing here? What did I hope to accomplish? Why was I standing in this passageway?

I was still facing the street and our house when I felt movement behind me. I turned to face a huge man in a faded blue suit—the head of the Jewish militia. I knew who he was, but because I didn't know what he would do with me, the blood rushed to my feet. Where did he come from? I wondered. Had he been stalking me every since I entered town? What was he doing here? A watchman in this graveyard? I felt dizzy, and my chest trembled with rapid heartbeats. When I recovered, I babbled. "What happened here? Where is my Grandmother? Do you know anything about my friends, the Hills?" But looking at him, I was instantly sorry that I had not run when I saw him, because his piercing stare, unmoving and crazed, sent chills through me. Finally, his gray face formed a grimace. "Verschwind," he whispered hoarsely. "Disappear! Be quick!"

Not wasting another moment, I brushed past him and ran down the uneven dirt path in the passage, returning where I had come from and passing all those deserted backyards and the empty houses of horror. I sped out of town, my legs working without let-up. I ran what seemed like miles before dropping to the ground, way past the spot where only a few hours earlier I had been robbed. Cradling my bruised feet, I sat without a single thought, just holding my feet, looking about me and weeping.

In the distance I saw farmers working their fields—a soothing pastoral. Warmed by the sun, hungry and tired, I fell asleep. When I woke up, the sun was gone, and it was dark and stifling. Heavy storm clouds moved rapidly above me, and with an explosion of thunder, rain fell like a waterfall. There were flashes of lightning at minute intervals, and each lasted long enough to show me where I was. I made a dash under a tree for protection from the rain, not stopping to think that it was not the place to be during a thunderstorm, and waited for the storm to pass.

When the rain slowed, and the thunder and lightning stopped, I began to walk slowly without giving any thought to which direction I was heading in. Suddenly I heard whispers, and at once two people grasped me, each by an arm, and pulled me into a clump of birches. At last I was with Mother and Father again. Breathlessly, anxious to get it all out quickly, I told them what I had experienced. They were too stunned for words, and without discussion or much thought, the three of us were on the road again, not knowing which way to go, but trying to get away from our farmer's field as quickly as our feet would carry us because we were no longer welcome. My parents told me the farmer's wife had brought no food that day, wanting us to be gone.

We walked until dawn, when Father knocked on the door of another paid farmer, Wladyslaw, an old friend of Father's family. This man was glad to see us and suggested we stay in his barn for a rest.

We were given a hot breakfast and tubs of water for baths, and later, while I slept, my parents spoke with Wladyslaw. When I woke up, I got the good news that I was to remain in his house as shepherdess while my parents looked around for a new town to settle in.

I was thrilled beyond words to have this place as my home for a while. Did I not love the country, I told them, and did I not always dream of living in the country? Did I not love animals and peasant food, and the woods, the rolling hills, and the fertile farmland bearing different crops? I rhapsodized. My face flushed with joy; I pressed both hands to my chest for fear my heart would jump out for sheer happiness. The four adults facing me smiled, and each had a different expression in his eyes. Father was sad to have to leave me behind. Mother was happy that I would have my dream come true, even if it was only for a short time, and the farmer and his wife looked at me with wonder. They were middle aged, married many years; they had no children, and they looked forward to the experience of having a daughter.

Their house was clean, showing signs of prosperity. The outside was whitewashed; inside, the rooms were painted pale blue. The very large front room was furnished in the usual way, with benches, a table, and a big hearth with many pots hanging from the ceiling, but the back room, small as it was, contained two mahogany beds, each with a large square feather pillow, covered in a starched white, hand-embroidered pillowcase, propped against its headboard. On the floor were scattered heavy white fur rugs.

The front of the hut, surrounded by a picket fence, had a garden full of snapdragons, hollyhocks, zinnias, sweet william, and many varieties of daisies. The stable held two cows and two horses. A goat, chickens, and geese were housed in a gray, weather-beaten lean-to. I loved everything about this farm.

Evenings there were the most cheerful of any I had experienced in the two and a half years past. The kerosene lamp was turned up high, and there was plenty of food, with milk and cheese in abundance. Wladyslaw and his wife sat at the table talking after each dinner, while I listened and hated to leave for my bed in the barn hayloft. During one of those evenings, I got a new change of clothes that was more suitable for a girl tending cows than the clothes I had worn when I arrived there. Does this mean that they like me and will ask me to be their daughter? I mused. A thrill went through me.

Sixteen

Because it was summer, hired help came in for daily work, often before daybreak. They usually took the tools they would need in the field and left. The stableboy slept in his own house, not at the farmer's. His work in the stables took about two to three hours; then he went to the field and worked there.

I was warned not to have long discussions with the help because my speech might reveal my identity. The farmer and his wife, should they be asked by anyone who might see me, would say I was a niece from the city spending part of the summer. I doubt that many locals believed this, but if they thought otherwise, no one said so, and my stay was uneventful from that point of view.

Thin, pale, and exhausted, I did not work the first several days. I slept most of the time, waking only to eat or when the farmer's wife called to take me with her in the field after her morning chores. There I watched the workers, sitting in the sun and frequently dropping off to sleep. Ordinarily it was unusual for me to sleep during the day—I only slept in daytime when I was ill—but I did not worry about this then, because I knew that I needed rest, and I had to take advantage of the opportunity to do so when I could to store up strength for what was to follow this idyll.

With anticipation, I started my official duties as shepherdess. It was a pleasant job. I took out the cows, the goat, and sometimes the horses to the meadow to graze when they were not needed for fieldwork or a trip to town. My day began before daybreak. As noon neared, I walked home, leaving my charges for as long as it took me to eat the big meal of the day. Immediately after dinner,

I went back to the meadow, often staying there until the sun was gone. I learned to tell the time by the position of the sun.

In just a few days, I knew Wladyslaw's fields like the palm of my hand. I knew that potatoes were its main crop. Walking behind the animals to pasture each day, I saw young potato plants as far as my gaze could reach.

On the days when I had the horses with me, I could hardly wait for dinner to be over so I could get back to pasture before anyone else returned to work. Then, when I was safely out of sight of the house, I would call to the chestnut mare to meet me at an old tree stump on which I stood waiting so I could climb up on her, bareback. Using my bare feet, I would give her a gentle kick, and she would take off, at first in a canter, then, as I urged her on, in a gallop for the woods. There, out of the sun and unseen by anyone, I would slow her down to a walk, and we would spend a few minutes enjoying a clandestine break in the daily routine.

This was not my first experience with horses. Father had taken me to Uncle Meyer's stable many times, where he had let me ride a pony or a slow horse, and I was beginning to like horses just as Father did.

Whistling for the mare to come to the stump was the greatest pleasure. When I gave the signal, she almost flew as if she knew that our time was limited, but in the wood, she was relaxed until we turned to go back. Then she would fly again, knowing we had to hurry. She rushed like the wind, her mane flying, while I, bent all the way forward, my arms around her neck, held on for dear life.

What joy these tiny outings gave me. In my mind, I pretended the horse was mine, and I wished I had something to give her in appreciation for all the pleasure she gave me. But I had nothing. No morsel of food, and certainly no cube of sugar. I could not walk out of the house with food in my hand. I was afraid someone would guess my secret. Perhaps no one would have minded, but

I was in such great need of necessities that taking this liberty without asking anyone's permission made me feel that I was doing something that would anger the farmer.

These joyful breaks were, by necessity, very short—ten, perhaps fifteen minutes long. I did not want to neglect my job, and I was anxious to please. I knew that the animals were perfectly safe by themselves. To wander off to someone else's field, they would have had to have been left alone for a long time. Wladyslaw's pasture was large; I could not even tell where the boundaries were.

Before I came, the cattle, that is the cows and the goat, were probably taken out to the pasture and left there for the better part of the day until someone came to herd them back home in the evening. The horses were being used too frequently to be taken that far from the house. They usually grazed near their stable. But when I arrived, they came along to graze in the large field whenever they were not needed.

Of course, the job paid no money, nor was it expected to. It provided food—I gained some weight and some strength with it and a hay bed. That was all I wanted. It also provided the good will of two dear people, and that meant more than anything else.

The experience of being this close to the land was new, and I found great satisfaction when, on rare occasions, I was asked to help with some planting. I could work with the earth. When I told my parents about this, they said they had never thought of me as a farmer.

I was only at Wladyslaw's a few days, but already buried deeply in some remote corner of my mind were the awful experiences of the recent past. I never thought of anything but the animals, my fields, and the food we ate. My appetite was as large as the stableboy's, who was twice my size and age. The clothing the farmer's wife gave me fitted loosely, but I knew that my own things would now be tight and uncomfortable. I started feeling self-conscious when men were around, but no one seemed to pay me any attention.

Sitting in the hayloft in the mornings, when it was still dark, I combed my hair, but I never looked in a mirror. I had none. Each morning as I left the barn, the farmer's wife waited for me with a basin of water. I washed hands and face. I planned to sponge bathe the rest of my body, but I kept putting it off until my parents came back, and Mother told me, in no uncertain terms, to wash from head to toe, including my hair, while she stood by and watched.

When I dropped my eyes to see the end of my nose, I saw freckles. I thought of Mother telling me once, a long time ago, when we still lived in Katowice, that with the first sign of freckles, I would have to start using a cream to prevent them from spreading, because it wasn't ladylike to have freckles. Why is this important? I wondered.

The time I was to spend at the home of Wladyslaw passed quickly, and lying near the roof of the barn one evening, I heard my parents enter. They had come to fetch me. All the time they were gone, they had wandered around looking for a place to live, visiting small towns and villages nearby, only to be disillusioned when most places they tried were already Judenfrei, with one exception—Pacanow.

Radwan

Seventeen

Pacanow was a town much like Dabrowa; it was situated a considerable distance from the village we were in presently, and some Jews still remained there. It was the only place we could go to.

We left the following dawn. There were no lengthy goodbyes, but I was so sad to leave that I was on the verge of tears for the rest of that day. Maybe it wasn't even any special liking I may have had for my temporary home; I remember being quite bored many of the afternoons as I lay in the grass watching the cows graze and having nothing to do, nothing to read, no pencil or paper to write on, no one to talk to. But it was the peace I felt on that farm—a safe haven—my spot in the hay at night way above everything and everyone, tucked away. It was that which I didn't want to give up, and I would have been willing then to make that farm my home for the rest of my life had someone offered it. I resented being a fugitive, of having to run and to hide, of not being able to admit who I was. And I was angry with my parents for taking me away from Wladyslaw's farm. What I did not know then, but what my parents later told me, was that even if they had been willing to leave me there, the farmer would not have wanted to keep me because his neighbors suspected me, and they had threatened to denounce him for harboring a Jewish child. So this pastoral interlude in my hurried life ended with a moist-eyed farmer's wife handing me a large package of bread, cheese, and hard-boiled eggs as we left.

Burdened with bundles of clothing, which Mother always

insisted on taking along "for a change, so that we won't look like beggars," we walked most of the day, passing villages where fieldworkers looked up at us but said nothing, knowing full well who we were. We passed Judenfrei towns, and although we looked conspicuous, these places were deserted, and we encountered no trouble there.

Twice stopping in the shelter of a birchwood or a clump of dense shrubbery, we rested and ate the food the farmer's wife had given me before we left. We drank water whenever we passed a stream and picked berries, which grew in abundance.

We reached Pacanow when the sun was setting. Father knew someone there, and we headed straight for a small house where the front door stood open, allowing the din inside to escape into the street. The house was crowded. Small children and a stout young woman with bushy black hair smiled at us as we entered. Wiping her hands on her apron, she shook hands with Father, then with Mother putting her arm around my shoulders, led me to a wooden table and handed me a plate with potatoes and a glass of buttermilk.

She smiled as she spoke, revealing a mouth full of gold teeth. I noted her swaying bust and hips as she walked, but my attention centered on my table companions. Around me sat about half a dozen grubby children, sipping their buttermilk noisily and eating potatoes with big spoons out of deep bowls. They eyed me intently, and I looked at each one separately, causing them to blush and giggle.

Father told the woman that we were homeless, and she immediately offered us her bedroom, which we accepted almost before she had finished making the offer. She told the story of how her husband had been killed several months ago, leaving her and her children to fend for themselves, and how she was trying to get along on what he had left her.

Pacanow remained one of about two or three little towns in that part of Poland where Jews were still allowed, and whenever another town became Judenfrei, the few Jews that were left would move to Pacanow or to the other available towns. This resulted in a population of big-city Jews, some still quite rich, and small-town Jews, many destitute. The original inhabitants of Pacanow were heavily thinned out through deportations and other akcjas, leaving empty houses available for new arrivals.

Originally, in a small town such as Pacanow, everyone knew everyone else, but now the population was so mixed, coming from many different places, that most were strangers. But we were strangers with a common bond—all equally persecuted. As a result, there was no snobbery. People stopped to speak with each other on the streets, discussing their experiences, their fears, and their estimates of what lay ahead for those who were left. Well-dressed, well-spoken children played with unkempt ones, sharing toys and food.

Food was, as ever, expensive and scarce. Farmers came to town surreptitiously, fearing they would be caught in an akcja. Potatoes were the mainstay of our diet.

The room we settled in was noisy. On the other side of our door, six children played late into the night and rose early each morning. With little supervision and no toys, they invented their own games, such as pulling each other's hair, tickling each other, or spitting to see who could spit farther or whose aim was best. Late evenings, when the noise subsided, the landlady would knock on our door to have a chat. If Mother answered (in whose presence she was shy and self-conscious), she would just look up and fold her arms over her bulging chest, asking if we needed anything or how we liked the room. Then she would end the conversation with a polite goodnight. When she spoke with Father, she was more forthcoming, letting out raucous peals of laughter in response to some of what he said.

Our first night there was discouraging to say the least. After turning off the light of the single bulb hanging from the center of the ceiling, Mother climbed into bed, where I lay waiting for her. Exhausted from the day's walk, Father snored gently on a nearby sofa. I was just beginning to sleep when I felt something crawl on my arm. Sitting up quickly, I asked Mother where the light switch was, but she was ahead of me, flooding the room with light to let us see what we already knew—the bed linens were crawling with bedbugs. The rest of the night was spent sitting in chairs, dozing fitfully.

As soon as she heard movement in the front room, Mother asked the woman for a pail of water and soap, and the cleaning started and continued for days: mattress airing, frequent linen changes, scrubbing the furniture and floors. Windows were left open day and night for days. It was a time before sprays and fancy cleansers. The only disinfectant was soap and water. Mother cleaned and scrubbed and changed bed linens until our nights became tolerable.

It was the end of August, and the heat began to lessen. I was on the way to the public well to fetch water when a man approached me. "Tell your father that the Germans have allowed a small ghetto in Dabrowa, and a number of Jews are living there," he said. "The ghetto is only on one side of Jagielonska Street, the side where your grandmother has her home. Across the street where you were living the houses stand empty and no one is allowed in them."

This was wonderful news, and even before I had filled my can with water, I turned and ran home to tell my parents that we could go back to Dabrowa. Mother, without losing a moment, started packing our few belongings, handing Father his jacket, where money was sewn into the lining, and while Father paid our landlady and went to the wells to look for the man who had sent the message, Mother put extra clothes on me. We were ready to leave, waiting only for Father to return from the public wells on market square. Father confirmed the news I had brought, and we cheerfully started on our way back home. The landlady walked with us for a bit, gave some directions to save us mileage, and offered us the room whenever we might need it.

We knew that the trek back would be long, but this seemed a mere trifle compared with what we thought awaited us at the other end of our journey. Comfort, clean clothes, a stove to cook on instead of the single hot plate Mother used to prepare our food in Pacanow, and, of course, roomy, clean beds. Yes, the trip back—mostly on foot with perhaps an occasional ride should a farmer offer us a lift on his horse-pulled wagon—was just a momentary nuisance. We were going home!

It was late night when we neared Dabrowa, or perhaps it was early morning, and history seemed to repeat itself: it was again thought best that I go into town to see if it was safe for us to go home. Leaving my parents in a thicket near town, I continued, a little afraid as I remembered the episode on my last reconnaissance. The road stretched before me clearly, lit by a full moon. I walked briskly, looking straight ahead, and as I entered town, I was stopped by the ominous, enduring silence. Remembering the gruesome scene I had encountered the last time I was here, when Dabrowa had become Judenfrei, I stood considering what to do. I was afraid to repeat that experience. Should I go on, I thought, or should I turn around and join my parents? Weighing this, I heard shuffling steps somewhere near, and not more than a few yards ahead, I spotted the figure of a bent old man, limping. I ran to catch up with him and after a greeting asked if he knew how many people were living in Dabrowa now. He didn't seem surprised at my presence. He picked his head off his chest to look at me, each eye a white blank, a whiteness that the moon only intensified. Startled momentarily, I looked into those deep sockets with their unseeing eyes and a thought flashed through my mind that I was lucky he could not see me. He would not know who I was.

Covered with sparse stubble, his chin touched the upturned collar of his shirt. "If you mean the Jews," he answered, "there are a few left, and they are all in the synagogue. There was a ghetto here for about two weeks, but that was only a trap to get them to come out of hiding. Just today they took all of them to the synagogue and told them they could live there." I asked if he knew any of the people who were now in the synagogue, and to my amazement he named my grandmother. Then he fell silent and walked away, leaving me to decide once more what to do.

I removed my shoes to avoid making a sound on the sidewalk and gradually made my way through back streets and alleys to the synagogue. When, from behind a building, I could see the sand-filled plaza on which the synagogue stood, I looked across to the entrance, where a single armed soldier was pacing.

Still behind the building, my mind working on how to get in touch with Grandmother, I kept looking at the sentry walking back and forth. I saw no one else. Concluding that since he was in front of the synagogue alone, all I needed to do was walk to the back of it, where I would be unseen. Once there, I would try to get someone's attention through the open windows. I was certain that not everyone inside was sleeping. I doubted, in fact, that anyone would be asleep in these circumstances.

Stalking along the walls of a few empty houses, I came to the edge of the plaza and waited for the soldier to turn so he would face away from my direction. When he did so, I ran swiftly without a sound across the sand to the back of the synagogue.

Beneath an open window, I heard the murmur of prayer. In a whisper I called out my grandmother's first and last names, and instantly a man's face appeared at the window while he called out to Grandmother.

When she saw me, her hands went up to her throat. "What are you doing here?" she whispered hoarsely.

"I came to tell you that we are in the wood, and we want you to come with us to Pacanow," I improvised.

"I can't get out of here. This is the end," she said. "You'd better run because if the soldier in front sees you, he will shoot you," she said frantically.

"Don't worry, he won't see me," I answered recklessly. "I want you to come with me now," I urged. "Climb out of the window, Granny." I was on the verge of tears, but she responded angrily, "Go away right now. Do you hear me? I cannot go with you. It doesn't matter for me anymore, but you, you are still young," her voice broke, and we both heard the soldier's heavy footsteps coming around the corner on the catwalk of the building.

Pressed against the wall, I slowly moved away from the window, then leapt into the sand and raced across it into a dark alley down the street to the end of town. When I felt safe, I slowed down to put on my shoes and continued, walking instead of running.

Way before I could reach the birch thicket where I had left them earlier, I gleaned the two figures of my parents waiting for me now that the moon no longer lit the fields as it had when I had started for town. They listened to my tale in silence, resigned. Mother mentioned something about her intuition warning her that things were not right. Father did not speak.

We decided to spend what was left of the night in a wood. Dead tired and hungry, we would spend the entire following day resting before starting the trek back to Pacanow. Another reason for wanting to remain where we were was the vague hope that somehow Grandmother would be able to leave the synagogue and find us in these woods.

It seemed that I had just a moment ago closed my eyes when I heard men's voices calling to us to leave. "You Jews, get out of here! We want no Jews here. Dabrowa is Jew-free, and that's the way we want it. Go, leave!" Father was about to start persuading them to let us rest for a while, but Mother tugged at his sleeve not to. We gathered our bundles—some clothing, some bread—and walked out of the wood into a field. It was overcast, and few farmers were working. We might have cut across the open field to save time, but Father insisted we take the long way through the dense pine wood so that no one would see us. There we could also pick berries for refreshment, he said. The narrow track that led down to where the pines were sparse also wound around the perimeter of the wood, and we walked along its edge. A short time later, we entered the field that belonged to the farmer who had let us spend two weeks at the beginning of the summer.

Hurrying before anyone caught sight of us, we made it to the barn and up to the roof. "Chances are," Father said, "that they won't even know we were here, and when it gets dark tonight, we'll leave for Pacanow."

We climbed the square bales of hay, layer upon layer, and I was first to reach the peak at the gable. Next came Father, and Mother followed. I lost no time burrowing a hole into the fragrant softness, and with complete abandon, fell into a deep sleep.

Gradually I felt someone taking me into a world of comfort and beauty: big chairs, soft carpets, delicious food. I luxuriated in an upholstered chair as I looked around a room full of beautiful furniture and paintings, letting my eyes wander around these mysterious surroundings. I stopped on the wall where a large painting depicted a tree in autumn, its leaves falling silently to the ground. I thought I heard a song accompanying this scene. I could not tell where the tune was coming from. I didn't recognize the room, nor did I know why I was there. Soon this faded and my eyes caught a grand piano in a corner on which invisible hands were playing early Beethoven. I sat transfixed, listening, but the notes inflicted pain, jabbing my skin as they passed, chasing each other until my entire body felt heavy, tormented.

I don't know how long I sat like this, but I finally realized that I was hungry, and I wanted to look for food. I could not move; my arms and legs felt as if they were made of lead. I felt fastened to the chair in which I sat. In what seemed no more than the flick of an eyelash, a table covered with white linen appeared before me, and on it were foods of all kinds, such as I had not eaten nor seen in a long time. I devoured untold amounts of food with ferocious speed, packing handfuls into my mouth, hardly giving myself time to chew before swallowing. When I had enough, the table disappeared magically.

I remained fastened to the chair I sat in and gazed out a darkening window, thinking of the approaching night, when I heard voices. Interrupting my reverie, I looked in their direction and saw several people playing cards. Suddenly a young man got up and moved toward me, removing his clothes as he walked. I felt a danger I could not classify. Then a voice like thunder announced in garbled language, "It is getting late. We shall go to bed." I was perspiring. I wanted to run, but the young man spotted me and pressed me back down into my seat, trying to put his arms around me yet somehow not being able to do so. I felt his breath on my face and his heavy hand on my shoulder.

When I opened my eyes, I realized that reality was no less dangerous than my dream had been. A man was shaking me and screaming into my face to get up and leave as fast as my legs would carry me. My parents, he said, were already gone, and I was to follow them or he would have the Germans come to get me.

I met Mother and Father a short distance down the road. We didn't talk. We headed straight for Pacanow. After a while, my parents told me how the farmer found out that we were in the barn. As she had entered the barn, Mother had dropped her bag on the hay at the door, and as soon as the farmer came into the barn, he spotted it. He knew at once that we were there. He started to scream for us to leave, but he had to climb to the very top before either of my parents woke, and no matter how hard they tried to rouse me by shaking and calling my name, I continued to sleep. Finally, they thought if they left, the farmer might allow me to stay, but he had made up his mind not to have any of us around. He was firm and final in his demand that we leave at once. He refused to listen to my parents' pleas to let us rest for the day.

We walked briskly, stopping only to pick berries or to buy bread and cheese at farms we were passing. We had only one goal now, one plan, to join the rest of the Jews in Pacanow and to be among them. Pacanow now appeared like a safe haven, though we knew full well that it would only be so for a short time. To escape the reach of the Germans no longer seemed in the realm of possibility.

We arrived in Pacanow late in the evening, and our room was awaiting us. Not bothering to unpack our meager possessions, all three of us dropped off to sleep fully clothed. We were awakened early the next morning by the landlady announcing that someone was looking for us. When Mother went out in the front room, she found Grandmother sitting at the table with a cup of milk with hot water.

Eighteen

Grandmother told us what had happened: Yesterday the Germans had taken the people who had been assembled in the synagogue and the Jewish militia among them and driven them all, under heavy guard, to the cemetery. There they ordered the militiamen to dig a large grave. When they finished doing that, they were told to stand around the grave. They were then machine-gunned into the grave while the rest of the assembly watched. Some of the men watching were ordered to throw earth over the bodies of the militiamen. That finished, the group was marched to market square, where they were to be loaded on trucks to be taken away. While walking to market, Grandmother escaped.

She could not recall how she did that, but she knew that she was suddenly passing her house, away from market square. She kept walking down Jagielonska Street, and when she reached the end of the sidewalk, she kept walking toward the villages and on to Pacanow. Grandmother had started that walk in the afternoon the day before she appeared at our door. She walked all night and part of a day to get to us. She was past seventy and had a permanent leg injury, which caused her to walk with a slight limp.

From Grandmother we found out that Uncle Emil and Aunt Franka had gone to Stobnica several weeks before the ghetto was established in Dabrowa. They hoped to be able to live there by obtaining Christian birth certificates and living under assumed names. When Uncle Emil and Aunt Franka left, Uncle Herman and Eva S. left together for unknown parts.

The four of us set up a home in our one room. Mother and Grandmother kept the room spotless. They cooked on the one round burner we had used during our previous stay there, and they were grateful to have electricity. They could have shared the kitchen stove with the landlady, she repeatedly made that offer, but they did not want to be in her way.

It did not bother us to live like this, and I never heard anyone utter a cross word. Our only wish was to be left alone in safety and to be able to die a "natural death in one's own bed." How many times did I hear Grandmother utter these words? It was not to be.

A few weeks passed quietly; then a terrible akcja took the lives of hundreds, leaving the rest of us in shock, paralyzed with anticipation of our impending end. Word spread that the Germans' final move when making Pacanow Judenfrei would be to remove the rest of us to concentration camp, a new concept, a new idea of where we would go when taken. Concentration camp. We now had a destination; it was no longer the unknown.

It took years of relentless horror to realize that the Germans were determined to exterminate all Jews.

My parents were not among those who, when warned before the war that terrible things were being planned for the elimination of Jews, believed that anything so horrendous as the total destruction of our people would come to pass. "How could that be," Father queried, "when we have lived here and been a part of Polish civilization for generations? Could Poland exist without the Jews?" He would laugh to make it sound like a joke, but he was dead serious. Now, resigned to the fact that Hitler would see to it that no Jew remained in Poland, Father said that if any of us hoped to survive this war, we would have to change our identity. It was possible, for large sums of money, to obtain Christian birth certificates. This, however, worked only for women, because at that time, in Poland, only Jewish men were circumcised. A Christian birth certificate was therefore nearly useless for Jewish men, Father said. A man could have the most meticulous set of Christian identification credentials, but once he was suspected of not being what he purported to be, he was stripped and examined.

Father's plan, then, was to give Mother and me (and Grandmother if she wanted it) new identities and help us settle as Catholics, the predominant Polish religion, in some town where no one knew us. Once that was accomplished, he would join the Polish underground, a sinister group composed of some Polish army officers and others. He expected no difficulty in joining because he knew some people in the underground, and being resourceful and in good health would make him a desirable member, he hoped.

Grandmother refused to be a part of our plan, saying she was not prepared to change her life at her age, come what may, but she did not object to Father's arrangement for Mother and me.

This plan, then, became Father's occupation for the next several days. He worked on it tirelessly day and night, laying the groundwork by gathering the necessary information, making contacts and appointments, taking trips to meet the people who could help.

Meanwhile rumors were rife of an impending end to our life in Pacanow. Pacanow would shortly become Judenfrei as were nearly all other towns in that part of the country. There would be no place for us to go.

The urgency Father felt now kept him away from home constantly until one day when he came home unusually early in a good mood, his ruddy face flushed, blue eyes sparkling. "You," he said facing me, "will have to go to Mielec tomorrow. There you will pick up the papers for your mother and yourself in Mr. Sz--ky's house. He knows that you are coming, and he is expecting you. When you leave here in the morning, you will go north out of town, where a farmer with a horse-drawn cart will be waiting to take you to Mielec."

I listened to his instructions carefully, taking in each word as he spoke, my excitement rising. Was it really true that we could—no, would—save ourselves? Mother and I living in some quiet apartment, each sleeping in her own bed in nightclothes? Could it be that our lives would take on some normalcy, that we would no longer live in an inferno? I was happy, proud of Father, excited that I would take part in executing his daring plan. I was filled with such joy as I had not felt in ages. I would live, and even better, I would have my mother with me.

Mielec had been Judenfrei for quite a while, so it was important that I have a totally Christian appearance. Before I left the house at dawn, Mother helped me dress. I wore my good green suit, pigskin sport shoes, and a white blouse. Knee-length white socks completed my outfit. Mother brushed and braided my hair, joining both braids in back with a navy blue taffeta ribbon. Inside my blouse, wrapped and tied in a white handkerchief, lay twenty-five thousand zlotys.

At the edge of town, a horse and cart waited. I approached, and the farmer called out, "Get in." I sat next to him on a wide board that served as a bench. We traveled at fair speed on the unpaved roads that connected all those small towns and villages, leaving a cloud of dust behind us and having quite a bit of it settle on our clothing. Conversation was not possible save for an occasional shouted word. The ride was noisy, as the wheels clattered against the bumpy surface of the road, and we were jolted from side to side. When we neared Mielec, the farmer let me off at the edge of town, telling me he would wait at the same spot where he let me off.

Wasting no time, I brushed off my clothes and pulled up my socks. Then, per Father's instructions, I proceeded in a leisurely manner to town. I was told not to give the impression that I was in a hurry. The streets in Mielec were empty of people, just as they had been in Dabrowa when I was there last. It was eerily quiet, an otherworldly atmosphere. No one lingered in a doorway here; no one waited for farmers to bring in food from the country. There was no fear, no panic—nothing. There were no sounds of mourning nor the drone of children cooped up inside their cramped houses. There were no people and no living sounds.

I looked at the address on a scrap of paper, then up at the sign on the street corner, and I knew at once where I was. Remembering the instructions given me by Father, I approached a small house on a deserted street with a luxurious garden in front. My knock brought a stout bald man to the door. Not waiting for me to speak, he said in a whisper, "You Josef's girl?" Infected with his voice, I whispered back, "Yes." "Wait here." He let me enter the vestibule as he disappeared inside for less than an instant. When he returned, he handed me an envelope, and his hand remained extended until I put the handkerchief with the money into it. Then, just as he was closing the door behind me, he whispered, "Your Aunt Franka got hers yesterday." "Where is she now?" I managed to inquire from behind the already closed door and heard him answer in a normal voice, "On the way to Berlin."

Still facing the door, I slipped the envelope where the money had lain before and buttoned my blouse. Then, turning to face the street, I retraced my steps to where the cart was waiting.

When Mielec was well behind us, I unwrapped the pancake Mother had put in the pocket of my jacket and bit into it with relish. As we neared Pacanow, we heard shots. At first I thought that I had imagined them, but the farmer confirmed hearing shots too, and as we moved closer, the sounds became more distinct. I wondered what to do, whether to continue on or to deviate onto the narrow path that led out to the fields, away from town. I didn't have to think for long; a decision was made for me by the farmer, who stopped the cart and refused to go farther. I got out and watched him go back in the direction from which we had just come. When I could no longer see him, I turned and headed to town.

Moments later, I heard the trot of a horse, and a wagon appeared before me. When I stopped to let it pass, the farmer and his wife asked if I wanted a lift. I accepted simply because I didn't know what else to do. When I was settled in back of them on the floor of the wagon, the woman started a conversation.

"Are you going to Pacanow?"

"Yes, and I am glad to be able to ride," I answered, only to be polite. I did not feel like talking. I was too preoccupied with what was happening in Pacanow, but she kept on chatting, and I clearly remember one of her comments when her talk turned to religion. "Soon," she said, "All religions will unite, and all the people of the world will believe in one God."

After hearing this, I understood why these two strangers had been so kind to me. They knew that I was just human, an equal regardless of what I might believe in.

About a kilometer before Pacanow, we met people fleeing the akcja. The farmer and his wife looked at me questioningly. I understood and told them to go on. I was determined to join my parents.

Getting off a few yards before the start of the town sidewalk, I headed slowly for my house in the ghetto as if nothing were happening. A German soldier saw me and, taking me for a Christian, shouted for me to leave. "Go home, you idiot, don't you see what is happening here?" I turned as if to leave town, but when I couldn't see him anymore, I ducked into the first open door I saw. The building was empty, and I was only a few houses away from where we lived, but it was not possible to continue. A storm of bullets and shrieks raged outside, and since I was already in the ghetto, I had to remain in hiding if I hoped to live.

Surrounded by the constant popping sounds of shots, accompanied by screams and moans, I skulked around this empty house, where through an open door the acrid smell of excrement, blood, and urine wafted in.

I don't know how long I stayed there, but when the noise subsided and the trucks could be heard leaving, it was almost dark, and trying to raise myself from the crouching position I had been in for so long, I felt stiff enough to have to wait a few minutes for the pain to ease. While I waited, I thought I heard movement. Listening intently and making no sound myself, I heard the faintest sound of a whisper. Someone else had saved his life here. I stood up and made for my house.

Mother, Father, and Grandmother were stretched out on beds when I came in. They looked at me as if I were something extraordinary.

"Why were you foolish enough to come back when everyone is trying to get out of here?" Mother said in a dour tone, her eyes unfocused. She had been treating me and addressing me as if I were her peer for quite some time now.

"Because I wanted to be with you," I answered simply taking the envelope from my blouse and handing it to Father. He looked at the papers inside it and said, "Good, good," before handing them over to Mother. Then, moving to the window and looking out at the town, where wagons manned by Jewish militiamen were being filled with dead bodies, he stood with his back to us without speaking.

"Sala's birth certificate says she is sixteen years old, but she is not even thirteen," Mother's voice interrupted the silence in the room as she looked in Father's direction accusingly. "What good will that do us? She cannot possibly pass for sixteen."

"You will probably never have to show her birth certificate to anyone," he answered tonelessly. "They are only interested in the adult, and once you have proven that you are a Catholic, they will take it for granted that your child is also Catholic." That ended the conversation because no one had the energy or the desire to talk. Sighing deeply, Mother put the envelope in her large leather bag, the same bag she had dropped in the farmer's barn, which had alerted him to our presence. Then she turned to Father once more. "I think you had better leave tonight. I want you to be the first to go, and I want you to remember that you have provided safety for me and for your daughter. Now, please, take some steps for your own safety."

Turning to look at all of us, he said, "I'll go now because now I may pass for one of the militiamen cleaning the streets. I'll walk out of town in comparative safety, and once the town is behind me, I'll remove the armband and head for the woods." He seemed to be saying this more to reassure himself than to tell us what he was going to do. With these words, wearing only the clothes on his back, he came over to Mother, brushed his mouth against her cheek, then shook hands with Grandmother, who all this time had sat on the edge of her cot, listening; then he kissed and hugged me and left the house.

I ran to the window to watch his husky frame disappear, and as sometimes happens, I was fully conscious of the fact that I would never see him again. Leaving the window, I joined the two sitting figures in the darkening room. My eyes remained dry.

When the noise of the cleaning wagons died down, there was complete silence for a while—no one and nothing moved anywhere. We were all in a trance. The heat and lack of air in our tightly shut room was oppressive. Mother, Grandmother, and I were lying on our beds clothed, dozing fitfully. My naps were filled with short, frightening nightmares, and when Mother woke me at dawn because she heard soldiers, I lay in a pool of sweat.

Soldiers were outside our windows. Soldiers were everywhere, and it was clear that the town was again surrounded, closed to outgoing and incoming traffic. We washed and freshened up, waiting for the light of morning. Grandmother had not spoken since the previous evening, and Mother uttered an occasional word only when necessary, both waiting for their destiny. I was gripped by fear, knowing that there was no escape this time.

The town quickly came to life. Voices were heard everywhere, and we saw through the windows soldiers assembling yesterday's survivors and marching them to the town's square. Mother made a bundle of underwear and another of bread and farmer's cheese, and when the pounding on the door came, we were ready to leave.

A peculiar sense of relief descended on us as we walked out of the house. We were ready to be taken—after weeks, months, years of nerve-shattering fear, of looking for places to hide, and of running around in circles. Without saying so, we each knew that it was a relief to be taken by them. We felt the relief of not having to plan strategies for saving ourselves that did not work and apparently could not work. The Germans now also staged forays into the country, combing fields and woods for victims. Trying to hide now meant prolonging the suffering, and we were glad to put an end to it.

We had no idea where we were being taken, but we hoped that now there would no longer be anything to be afraid of. We refused to believe that we were being taken to our deaths, even though some of the people in the transport knew that and talked about it openly.

"Raus!" was the only word the soldiers screamed, standing at the open door, and the three of us were on the way to the market along with the rest of the town's survivors.

Our landlady and all her children had gone the day before. Thus, I, holding Mother's hand, and she, holding her bundle and her large leather bag with our Catholic birth certificates inside it, marched, the sun burning our foreheads. Grandmother walked a few steps behind because of her ailing left leg, which would not allow her to keep pace with us. I kept looking back, making sure she walked straight. I feared more than anything to have to witness the death of a relative, and knowing that the Germans didn't send away the old and the sick, I worried that one of them would spot her limping and shoot her. But, although a little slow, she walked straight, making a supreme effort to look well, and it seemed good enough for the soldiers not to notice her small infirmity.

I felt my heart weeping for Grandmother and for Mother, who looked so tired and gray. We had now been running for so long that I began to have moments when I thought we deserved this punishment; otherwise why would it last so long? The Germans' indoctrination about the worthlessness of Jews was beginning to take hold. Yet, when I tried to find reasons for this unflagging persecution, I could reconcile it with nothing I knew of. We have never, as a people, done anything to deserve this cruel punishment, I reasoned. Our only crime was being Jewish.

In the square we joined waiting crowds and others who were being herded in from every corner of town. We were not allowed to sit, and we stood waiting to be loaded on trucks. Grandmother was tired, but she dared not sit. Several old people had already been shot because they had complained of tiredness and thirst. An old lady sat down on the cobblestones to rest her swollen legs, and a soldier immediately shot her in the head. She fell head first, the rest of her body forming a mound, with only a thin trickle of blood touring its way out from under her.

Some groups of people in the square were herded in from other places, other towns and surrounding villages. They looked exhausted. And while the square was teeming with humanity, the surrounding streets bore no signs of life, and the hundreds gathering here presented an eerie spectacle as they spoke in whispers—even infants only whimpered, not daring to raise their voices. The only loud voices were those of the Germans, barking out orders. Mostly, people stood around without talking, shifting their legs, perspiring, and waiting—for what? No one really knew for sure what the second act in this drama would be.

We had been given no food or drink, and by this time the sun stood high, bathing the square and its inhabitants. I was very warm in the jacket of my green wool suit, which I had now worn two days and a night, and the extra sweater Mother had made me put on, anticipating our trip to last into fall, but I kept on all my clothes, not daring to make an unusual move.

About midafternoon, we were told to form ranks of four. That accomplished, we started moving. We were not told where we were being marched, but some recognized the way to Szczucin. The three of us—Grandmother, Mother, and I—and a young woman whom we did not know formed our rank of four. I walked somewhat in front of Grandmother to protect her from the sight of a soldier, because she now limped badly. Mother hardly spoke, and I could see that she too was tired and on the verge of collapse. She held the bundle with our underwear in one hand and the large brown leather bag under her arm, still hoping for a future, the basis of which lay in that bag. She left the package with food on the square—we were not hungry. We walked in silence.

Looking at the length of the line of people, I estimated the number of people in the transport to be more than two thousand, but it did not look as if all of us would reach our destination. Soldiers walked on both sides of us, carrying rifles with bayonets at their ends, ready to dispose of those who appeared unable to walk. Many small children were picked up on those bayonets and thrown in the ditch that ran along the road because they cried. There they would remain to die while their parents had to walk on.

So many people were shot during the march that isolated riots broke out sporadically, creating enough confusion to keep the soldiers busy in those places where they occurred. Watching them gather where the disturbances required their presence gave me an idea that I at once communicated to Mother. "I want to live. I am too young to die," I said to her several times. She looked at me expressionless, her eyes hooded. I turned to Grandmother and whispered my plan to her. I would run away from the transport when the next riot broke out and the soldiers were too busy to watch us closely.

Grandmother said to go ahead and to take Mother with me. "How are you going to do this?" she asked in a whisper. "I am just going to step out of line and fall into the ditch—afterwards I'll crawl out into the fields," I said under my breath. For the first time, the young woman in our row spoke, "I'm with you," and Grandmother added, "Leave me out. I'm too tired. I'll only be a burden."

Now that I knew what I would do, and reassured by Grandmother's support, I began to look out for an opportunity to get out of line without being noticed. First, we rearranged our rank. I switched places with the young woman, who was on the outside. Then came Mother, whose hand I held. The young woman was third, and Grandmother took the last spot at the end of the rank. Mother dropped her bundle of underwear and hung her bag over one shoulder. We continued to walk.

The soldier guarding us on the side of the ditch coughed and spit constantly into a large green handkerchief as he walked looking ahead, seemingly paying no attention to us. Time was passing, but our position had not changed—we walked, a heap of ragged humanity, dragging itself across the parched road, the sun burning into the overheated, overdressed marchers going past cozy homes and flower gardens. Soldiers with bayonets at the ends of their rifles walked on either side of us.

I became impatient, and I suddenly realized that I could not wait for another riot. A few yards ahead I noticed a farmhouse we would soon be passing. I looked up at the soldier, who, stone faced, looked straight ahead, then looking at Mother and the young woman, I inclined my head slightly and like a flash of lightning moved out of line, pulling Mother who pulled the young woman along with her, leaving Grandmother to march on.

We were instantly in the ditch, then climbing out the other side of it and running toward the farmhouse, along its fence and on out to the open field. We knew that our chances of getting away were small. Too many armed soldiers could see us from the road. But we had nothing to lose, and they could not easily stop the march to pursue us. Bullets began to fly around our heads as the Germans fired, and one of them ran after us, yelling, "Halt!" which we ignored while we continued to run in the direction of a wood. When the shooting stopped, we slowed down and turned to look. The transport was now barely visible, and our pursuers were gone.

A grimacelike smile crossed Mother's face. Then we sat down beneath some trees for a moment's rest. The sun was nearing the earth, and the last light of day began to fade. The young woman asked what we would do next, but Mother had no answer; none of us knew what to do. The young woman (we didn't know her name) said she would stay in the wood for a day or two, and not wanting to stay in an open field any longer, left with a brief goodbye.

Mother and I remained sitting while she took out the Catholic identification papers from her bag and looked them over carefully. "You are Christina," she said, pointing to my new birth certificate. She looked at her own after a while, but she said nothing. I felt strange things as we sat together under a tree, looking at these papers. We had escaped our captors. We were alive, free, and we had Christian identification papers. What I felt was something like happiness veiled in desperation. What I felt was momentary relief.

I don't know what Mother felt. She did not speak. We looked at each other, and I said nothing. I knew that she was thinking of a plan for us, and I waited. Suddenly, I said urgently, "I want to go in the same direction as the transport. Even if we were to catch up to them, no one would recognize us. There are too many people marching to remember us. And we can now prove that we are not Jewish, you and I, Mother, and once we get to Szczucin, we can look for a place to live. We can settle in a Judenfrei town and be finished with all our troubles."

She pondered what I said for an instant but shook her head. "I don't want to go to Szczucin. I want to go back to Pacanow." I knew that I would not go back to Pacanow and at the same time realized the importance of agreeing with Mother. She was all I had left. How could I survive alone? Therefore, when I spoke, it did not seem as if I were the one speaking, but some stranger inside of me. Quietly, gently, afraid of what reaction my words would elicit, I said, "I don't think I want to go back to Pacanow. I don't think I can do it. I don't know why."

Again she looked at me without speaking, and I looked back at her and saw that she was not angry nor disappointed that I did not want to do what she wanted me to. I felt that, without saying so, she was leaving the responsibility for myself to me, and that she would not insist that I go to Pacanow. So I was not surprised to hear her say, "If you feel like going to Szczucin, then go ahead. I am going to Pacanow. I think you understand that in these times, we must each act according to the dictates of our own minds, and we must use our own judgment, because some of us are destined to survive all this, and some are not."

Never before had I been given such complete responsibility for my actions. But I understood that now, when the question was one of life and death, Mother being anxious for me to save myself and uncertain of her fate—perhaps even tired of living in these difficult circumstances—had turned the decision of my next move over to me.

Given the freedom to make the decision without Mother's support left me momentarily speechless, but I soon recovered, and having firmly decided to go to Szczucin, I said as I got up, "All right, I'll go if you promise to meet me tomorrow near Szczucin so we can look for a place to live." "I will," she said. "I will meet you at the city limits tomorrow whenever I can get there, but for now, I am going back to Pacanow."

We took a last look at each other, then removing a light wool square from her neck, she tied it around my hair, and without another word we turned, each in her direction, leaving an ever-growing distance between us as we walked away. I did not look around to see her walk away, and I don't know if she turned to watch me. The scarf she put over my hair is the only material thing I have left of my life with my parents.

Nineteen

My legs hurt terribly, and I made straight for the road to see if I could get a ride to Szczucin. A farmer with a big load of hay pulled up and offered to take me there for five zloty. I had not thought of money until that moment. I looked in my pocket, where I found three five-zloty bills. I got on the wagon, he cracked his whip, and we moved ahead.

I had nothing but the clothing on my back, and I knew now that I possessed ten zloty. I felt strangely at peace, and being off my feet added to the feeling. No transport, no bullets, no Germans, no bundles to carry—nothing. Unfettered, I lived for the moment and did not think of what I would do in an hour, or less, when we reached Szczucin.

Nearing town, we heard the cries. At first I felt nothing. As we came closer to the railroad station, our passage was blocked by the part of the transport that had not yet reached its final destination. The road was crowded with people and soldiers, and the farmer pulled over to the side of the road and waited until the marchers had reached the railroad tracks behind a chainlink fence.

On the track stood a freight train. Each red boxcar had small barred windows on the front and back walls, high up, near the roof. One boxcar had its door wide open on one side only, which looked like a gaping mouth ready to devour whatever came its way.

I looked at that miserable mass of humanity as we passed, trying to find Grandmother, but the confusion was too great to be able to spot a familiar face. Most marchers were wailing pitifully; children were hysterically looking for their parents; women begged for water; and some called out to the farmer to take them away. I suddenly realized that I was in danger, sitting exposed in back of the wagon, where everyone could see me. What if someone were to recognize me and call out my name? But night had nearly fallen, and the darkness shrouded the scene and gave me protection.

I don't know what the farmer thought of this pandemonium, and I was glad that I sat in back, separated by the load of hay. I wanted no conversation. I did not want to be seen or looked at in my grief and in my fear. I thought again of Grandmother. Was she looking up at the wagon? Did she spot me in the hay? Would anyone else recognize me, or was everyone too intent on their wretchedness to raise their gaze to the road?

"Hurry," I called out to the farmer. "I have to be home before it gets too late." "Where do you want to get off?" He asked, not looking around. "At the next corner," I said without thinking. A moment later I was on the pavement, hurrying ahead, not knowing where to—without destination. I walked as fast as my feet would carry me until I reached the other end of town. There I stopped and looked around me. All was quiet. I felt that I must keep going until I reached the country. I neared a farmhouse, where a light went on before I got to it; I knocked and was let in. Parents and children—a family—looked me up and down and asked no questions. I asked if I could spend the night in the barn, to which the answer was yes. Nothing else was said, and for the moment, I did not volunteer anything.

I think I presented an obvious picture. Without asking, I was given black bread and a bowl of hot milk, and as I ate, I slowly told them what I had gone through that day. They wanted to know more about the transport, and I told them that it was at the railroad station in Szczucin, waiting to be shipped out. "In that case," the man in the family said, "they will pass here, because the railroad tracks are only about a hundred yards away from our house." After that, he turned down the wick in the lamp, and we sat around the window, waiting for the train to pass.

It wasn't long before he stood up and leaned out the open window, saying, "Here they come." His wife and daughters moved closer so they could see better, while I stood behind them, all of us looking into the darkness, waiting for the train.

It approached slowly, moving as if it could not bear its load. It traveled in total darkness. Only the locomotive bore some light. The rest of the cars were not lit on the outside nor the inside. As it approached, we heard the shrieks and lamentations of the people packed inside.

I moved away into a corner of the room and sat there listening. I felt as if invisible hands were tearing at my body. What was I doing in this house, in this room with these strangers? I belonged on that train with my people.

Creeping, the train took quite a few minutes to pass, and when the last sound died away and everything was quiet again, I walked out of the house without a word and went toward the barn. I let myself in, and a few minutes later, I heard the farmer latch the door from the outside. I did not worry about what would happen to me here. Would the Germans find me? Would the farmer inform them? I did not care. I lay for what seemed like hours in a burrow, surrounded by hay, thinking of Grandmother. Was she one of those who had cried out in that train as it passed? I thought of Mother. Where was she now? I'd have to leave early in the morning to meet her. And Father—where was he? What was he doing? Would I ever see him again? When oh when would that be? When would we all be together again? Staring into the darkness, I was too busy with my thoughts to sleep.

For one of my birthdays, Father had given me a gold ring with a ruby, surrounded on either side by tiny diamonds. As I waited for sleep to come, I played with my ring, sliding it up and down my finger until it fell into the hay. I felt a momentary loss, but I knew I should not worry about it. I remembered what Mother had said when the Germans took Aunt Raisa's house away from us: "Never get so attached to anything that you can't leave it behind." I have lived by that motto ever since.

I seemed to have slept only a few minutes when I awoke, and indeed, it may well have been only a brief nap, but the first light of day was already creeping in through the cracks in the barn. I climbed down from my hay bed and looked out through the tiny window. No one was up, and it looked like it might be five o'clock. The door was latched on the outside, which meant I could not use it to leave, and I did not want to stay longer because I was anxious to meet Mother at the other end of town, which was better than an hour's walk.

Struggling at the small window, I succeeded in pushing myself through. On the soft dewy grass, I wetted my hands and face and straightened my clothing. With my fingernails, I brushed the hay out of my hair. Before me stretched a field and the pale morning sky. I took a deep breath and thanked God for keeping me alive; then, walking briskly, I reached the other end of Szczucin by the time day had fully dawned, but I kept going, keeping my eyes straight ahead of me and hoping to find Mother coming toward me or perhaps waiting for me. I had covered quite a distance, but Mother was nowhere to be seen. I finally sat down at the edge of the road and waited. Nothing stirred—there was no one anywhere. What a contrast to yesterday's tumult.

Not taking my eyes off the direction from which Mother was to arrive, I began to doze, and when after a while I was roused by the sound of a horse's neighing, I stood up and started again in her direction. I would meet her, I thought. I kept my head down while I walked because I wanted to be surprised by her sudden appearance. I walked slowly, waiting to hear her call out to me.

Maybe she would call out my new name, the one on my new birth certificate. I would then lift my head, and she would be before me. Though I took my time, I had already covered half the distance to Pacanow, passing some corpses that had been lying there since the day before, and pools of dry blood here and there where a corpse might have already been removed.

As hope of seeing Mother began to ebb, an indescribable loneliness took hold of me. I felt as if I were the only living person in a world of the dead. I wondered why I was living, what for, and once more regretted having escaped the transport. I had already forgotten the fear and the panic of yesterday, when even at the risk of instant death, I wanted out of the march. Yesterday—when all that mattered was staying alive.

I began to run. Was this fear, this feeling of abandonment, not worse than yesterday's panic? Which was worse? I didn't know. I couldn't think. I wanted to walk forward, ahead, to keep moving, running from all this, away from everything. Where was Mother? Why wasn't she here? I felt bereft because I knew I would not get my mother back. I searched the emptiness around me, trying to draw her out of the landscape. But I knew then that she would not come, just as I had known I would never see Father again when I watched him disappear down the street.

When I got to Pacanow, I heard voices echoing in the streets. I headed for the market. I could clearly make out what was being said because there were no other sounds. The streets were deserted, eerie. I was by now used to this kind of atmosphere, having encountered it so many times before. The open houses, the creaky sounds of emptiness. I knew what I heard was the Jewish militia cleaning up after yesterday's deportation. I went to the square and to my complete surprise found Uncle Emil working with the rest of the healthy, able-bodied men picked by the Germans for cleanup. He traveled with that group of men from town to town as each became Judenfrei, to clean up the dead left behind, collecting the bodies and burying them in communal graves.

When he caught sight of me, he stepped away from the group and motioned me to follow him. We walked up some concrete steps into the hallway of a building and moved farther in so as not to be seen. His whisper was desperate; his eyes showed fear. "Why are you here, little one? Don't you know that the town is Judenfrei?"

"I know it," I whispered back. "But I thought I would find Mother here." I looked up at him questioningly and, without saying it, implored him to tell me that she would meet me here later. I wanted my uncle to produce my mother for me.

"She was here yesterday, right after the transport left, and she decided to keep walking to Stopnica. There are still some Jews left there." He said this quickly, anxious to finish our conversation, afraid a German would come looking for him.

"Didn't she say anything about me? Leave a message?" I asked bitterly.

"She said you have a better chance to survive without her." He began fishing in his trouser pocket.

"Where is Aunt Franka?" I asked.

"In Berlin by now."

"How did she get there?'

"With her Christian passport and birth certificate, she took the train to Busko-Zdroj. There she went to the Arbeitsamt [the German bureau of work] and volunteered for work in Germany." He handed me a fifty-zloty bill and said, "Take this, you will need to buy a meal, but now you have to go. If you are caught here, you will be shot without a moment's hesitation."

I looked at his ruddy face and his sturdy body. I looked at the tweed knickers and remembered the wonderful times we'd had when I was little, in Katowice, the stories he loved to make up and tell me and the money he always put in my hand: "Buy with this what your mother won't let you have." He would wink, then take me off his knees. Years of happiness flashed through my mind. How different he was now, tense and afraid, concerned for his safety and mine. He wanted me to leave, wanted to be rid of me.

I put the money in my pocket and walked back to the open door, leaving Uncle Emil where he stood. Looking out in every direction to make sure no one was watching, I jumped off the steps and turned to my left—the direction from which I had come a few minutes ago. Minutes that held an eternity.

I walked to Szczucin without thinking, without knowing what I was doing nor what I should be doing. When I almost reached that town, a horse and wagon caught up with me, and the farmer called out to get off the road because a transport was being led to the railroad station in Szczucin. I asked where the transport was coming from, and he said that it was from Stopnica. My knees gave way under me, and I crumpled into the grass. But at once propelled by what seems now like inhuman strength, I was up again and headed for a nearby wood. When I reached a spot I thought to be safe, I stopped and waited for the transport to pass. Would I see Mother among all those marchers?

The same screams and cries accompanied this transport as yesterday's. It was an instant replay of yesterday's events. Hypnotized with fear, I watched from my hiding place in the wood, and the pains in my legs and the grumblings of my stomach were the only reminders that I was alive. The performance on the road was identical to yesterday's: half-dressed, whining children, complaining mothers, soldiers with their fixed bayonets at the ready. I watched intently, knowing that Mother was among these people, but I did not see her. It was all a blur.

It is not only possible, it is probable that Mother was in that transport. Having entered Stopnica sometime toward early morning, probably when the akcja was already in progress, hungry and tired beyond imagination, and no doubt a little confused from lack of sleep, she would have been an easy target. Had she had her wits about her, she could have easily identified herself with her Christian papers. Maybe she tried. On the other hand, in her condition, she may have been ready to give up, as her comment to Uncle Emil, that I had a better chance of surviving without her, might have indicated.

I never saw her again, nor did I ever hear from her after our parting on the edge of the wood on that late summer afternoon. Our Christian papers, on which Father had worked so hard, remained in Mother's big brown leather bag, unused.

Twenty

I waited until the transport was well out of sight, then continued on my journey through the woods, away from the main road. I became strongly conscious of the fact that I was an escapee and had to avoid people as much as possible. Looking for food, I formed a strategy: I would visit each farmer my father had paid in advance in case we needed shelter. But I would not simply ask for help; I would offer to do any kind of work they had. In that way, perhaps I had a chance of being kept on as a hired hand, rather than as just a parasite needing food and a roof over my head.

As this plan took shape, my emotions lifted somewhat, and I stopped here and there to pick whatever berries were still left on the bushes. I even ventured near some farms to pick the fallen fruit from under apple and pear trees.

The first farmer I visited chased me away, calling out after me not to come back. He had no use for Jews. Toward evening I felt so depleted that I thought I might soon die anyway, but seeing a little hut at some distance, I decided to try again. Making my way toward it, my spirits rose. I had hope. In response to my knock, an old woman opened the door—would she give me something to eat, I wondered. She did. Sitting outside on her stoop, eating the bread and milk I got, I savored the grainy taste of the bread, washing it down with the soothing warmth of the rich, sweet milk. After the meal, I walked back into the wood and, propped against a tree, instantly fell asleep.

I woke the following day when the sun was already high. I did not know where I was nor how I got there. My first thought was to comb my hair. I meant to look presentable. But I had no comb. I untied Mother's scarf and the wilted taffeta ribbon from my braids and ran my fingers through the long tangles until all the kinks were out; then I made one braid starting at the nape of my neck and tied it again with the blue taffeta ribbon Mother had braided into my hair when I'd left Pacanow to pick up the Christian papers in Mielec. How many days ago had that been? A week, two weeks? Could it be that it was only three days ago? How time stands still sometimes.

I took off my jacket and shook it out to free it of the pine needles that stuck to it, straightened my socks, and tied my shoes neatly. Refreshed, I left the wood.

My stomach growled, and I began to look for a farm where I might get something to eat. I looked around as far as my eye could reach and beheld with wonder and longing the few scattered white huts surrounded by their gardens. I clearly remembered the reception I had gotten in one farmhouse, and I almost lost the nerve to ask anywhere else, but nature was stronger than my resolve, and soon I neared the first hut and headed for the door. Afraid and full of foreboding, I knocked. Horrors, it was the same place where the farmer, yelling and cursing, had slammed the door in my face the day before.

Today, however, a woman answered my knock. "Oh, it's you again," she said, not unkindly. "Yes," I whispered. Could she use someone to do chores around the house? I inquired. Did she need a shepherdess? I knew all about livestock. Out of the question; she could not keep me. She would give me food, but then I would have to go, before her husband got back.

So it went for weeks. I didn't keep count, one day ran into the other, nights into days and days into nights. I lived in the woods, unaware and most of the time unafraid of the dangers it might harbor. Not every night was easy. I remember many a night lying awake until dawn while my imagination played tricks on me, but I was never hurt by any animal, and I realized then that I need only fear people. Other nights, lying on its soft floor, I listened to forest noises until I was lulled to sleep.

To fill my time during the day, I hid behind shrubbery, studying various ferns. I judged the time of day by the position of the sun. I observed cloud formations and began to understand the workings of weather. I thought most of my days were alike, but I would have liked to have kept a diary. I realized that in that sameness there was significance. But I had no pencil or paper. Instead, I started making mental notes of things that had happened before I was left alone, with the plan of writing down as much as I could as soon as I could. I thought of my old diary, which was probably still lying among my schoolbooks in our house in Dabrowa, and I mentally compared it to a future diary--they would be very different.

Ever vigilant for possible danger, I did not stay in one area but kept moving. After a while I did not know where I was. Mostly I wandered around in a haze, thinking that I had a goal, a destination, but when I tried to think where my destination lay, I could reach no clear point. Hopeful thoughts were with me each day, but I did not really know what I was hoping for. Time was passing, and my situation remained the same. I begged for food, managing one, two meals a day. The meals usually consisted of bread and milk or potatoes and buttermilk, which I learned to love, and sometimes millet with milk. There were no streams where I wandered, and I remember being thirsty much of the time. For drink, I depended solely on the milk that was a part of my daily meal. I saw many of the precious mushrooms Mother and I had coveted when we were gathering them near Dabrowa, but I did not pick them because they had to be cooked to be eaten.

Hunger was my steady companion. Sometimes I imagined smelling delicious food being cooked, and I followed the smell only to have it dissipate into thin air. Hunger made me aware of myself. "Who am I," I thought, "that I have no food to assuage my hunger? Who am I that I sleep in someone's field? Who am I that I have no one, that I wander alone, friendless, waiting for someone to take pity on me?"

Alone, bare of possessions, without a home—I loved life. Bewildered and frightened, I rejoiced in the beauty of nature. My clothing began to show wear. I had to discard the torn socks I wore because they spoke of who I was. What girl who had a home would wear socks with such big holes in them. Not even the poorest peasant child. They might be darned, but they would not be torn. I still had illusions of being well dressed, and clearly torn socks did not go well with the rest of my outfit. Giving up my socks made my feet cold, especially at night. The weather had already changed; nights were cold, and days were often cloudy and damp. I thought it was the end of October.

Something else began to trouble me, but it was not as easily disposed of as a pair of torn socks. I was uncomfortable in my sweater. I thought at first that I was becoming allergic to wool, but I soon discovered that it was nothing of the sort. My sweater was filled with lice, and to get relief from itching, I developed the habit of swishing around the upper part of my clothing. As if this plague were not enough, these pests also found their way into my hair.

Roaming the countryside and the woods, I had, by now, completely lost track of time, but something that occurred unexpectedly roused me into action. I woke one morning to find the ground outside the wood covered with snow. Although it was still warm in the wood—I could quite comfortably lie in my shelter, watching dust motes do their slow dance in the long shafts of sunlight that filtered in between the conifers—once out in the open, a sharp wind gripped me, turning my skin to gooseflesh.

As terrible as this may have seemed at first, it turned out to be a blessing in disguise, because it made me realize that to survive the winter, I would have to find shelter. I did not go begging that morning; instead, after surveying the white expanse from the edge of the wood, I turned back across the soft carpet of pine needles and sat down with my back against the tree where I had slept. I would make myself presentable, I thought, and then decide what to do. With all the sleep I had gotten lately, I had energy, but I was very thin with lack of food. Yet, I was sufficiently stimulated to be able to plan ahead. My mind was clear and reasonable. I seemed to have woken from a long, deep sleep, and while I picked lice out of my sweater, I decided on a course of action.

First, I would orient myself to my whereabouts. After that, another thought would come. But one thing remained uppermost in my mind: if I hoped to live, I could not remain in the wood, because I would freeze to death. Now, sitting under the tree that had lately been home, I waited for the sun to shrink the snow, which would make it possible for me to leave my shelter without being too conspicuous. A lone figure in a green suit against the white background—I wore no stockings or gloves—I would stand out too much. I did not want to take that chance.

All these weeks, living as I did, I still thought that I blended with the peasant folk living in the area, not for a moment realizing that all who saw me had to know, without a doubt, that I was hiding out.

It was warmer and the snow was melting when I left the wood. I paid careful attention to all landmarks as I walked, looking for familiar signs. After a brief walk, I recognized the village I was in. It was Radwan, a village not very far from Dabrowa. During those weeks alone, I had not realized I was moving away from Szczucin and Pacanow. And now, finding myself near my home, in familiar surroundings, gave me courage. I knew there was no question of ever returning to Dabrowa, but just being near it warmed me.

I kept looking around the fields as I walked and thought I recognized them even though they were now barren, with the crops all gone. I had never before wandered in these villages in winter. And I realized now that the different areas where I had slept in recent weeks were the same woods where I had spent many wonderful days—first with Mother as a young child, then with Alfred and the rest of my friends. I wished that I had known this sooner while I had wandered around alone; it would have given me comfort to know I was in those once happy places.

Radwan was one of the villages where Father had paid farmer Stanek to give Mother and me shelter in case we needed it. I recalled what Father had said: "In Radwan, look for farmer Stanek's hut. He will help you."

Of all the other villages and tiny hamlets where I had spent so much time trying to escape the massacres, the only name I remember is that of Radwan. I did not write any of those names down in my improvised diary. Along with Wladyslaw, Farmer Stanek of Radwan is the most remembered name.

I knocked on a familiar door and was let in. With harvest over, everyone was home: man, wife, daughters, and a young son. Farmer Stanek asked about my parents, and when I told him what had happened, he at once wanted to know what I planned to do. I said I didn't know. Having been rejected so consistently in so many places, I did not dare ask him to let me stay, uncertain of even the interest he was showing and not entirely trusting his apparent kindness.

Rising from the bench on which he sat, he tapped my shoulder and motioned me to follow him into the vestibule. He did not want the others to hear what he had to say. His suggestion saved my life.

"Listen carefully to what I'm saying and don't interrupt until you've heard everything," he began while I looked up at him, a lightheartedness creeping into me as he spoke.

"You will go to Germany to work. They are supposed to send for my daughter this month, but if you go to Tarnów, using her name, they won't call for her, because they will think that she has already gone of her own will."

With most men gone to war, Germany was in dire need of workers. Women were doing what was then considered men's work, and men and women brought in from occupied countries filled menial jobs and worked in factories.

When he finished, I stood speechless. I had not been with people in many weeks, and I had seen no Germans. How could I face this complicated plan now? I did not think I could go out into a totally Christian world pretending that I was somebody I was not. How could I possibly go to a city like Tarnów—long Judenfrei—and register in a German Arbeitsamt for work in Germany, willingly? I did not feel capable of facing people, much less of pretending to have another name than my own, another religion, different parents.

For more than two years now, survival had been the uppermost consideration in my mind, but now that a time had come for taking the final deciding step, I was bewildered by the plan before me. I didn't think I could manage it.

The farmer knew what I was thinking, and he tried to reassure me. "Don't worry, no one will recognize you. You will give them this address and Eva's birth date. Your looks will help you pass for a Christian." Looking me up and down, he continued, "You only need to comb your hair."

What alternative did I have? This not only seemed like a good plan, it was the only plan. Still, I was so frightened I literally shook. His voice broke the spell. "Now come to where it's warm and let us give you some food." He put his arm around my shoulders, guiding me back into the room where his family sat around the hearth. "You will be just fine, Eva," he said in a loud voice for all to hear. He was calling me Eva. I did not look up, thinking he meant his daughter.

I was given a bowl of water and soap. I washed my hands and face—for the first time in weeks. I asked for a comb so that I could work on my hair.

Having finished that operation, I was given food. While I ate, the farmer wrote on a slip of paper his daughter's birth date and handed me the slip. Eva's age gave me another scare. She was sixteen years old, and I was nearing thirteen, or at least I thought I was nearing thirteen. By the change in the weather and the shortness of the days, I figured it must be October, and I may possibly have passed my thirteenth birthday, which fell on October 13. But even if I were thirteen already, I knew I did not look sixteen. Surely, I thought, someone would catch that. Not wanting to raise further doubts for fear the farmer would change his mind, I took the paper, folded it neatly, and put it in my pocket. The farmer wished me luck, and I saw that I was expected to be on my way. I was taken aback by such a quick dismissal. I expected to spend the night and start on this long trip in the morning. But he seemed in a hurry to see me go, either because he wanted to ascertain his daughter's safety by wanting me to get to Tarnów as soon as possible, or because he simply didn't want me around. At any rate, I had a plan now—a goal—and a long journey before me, and it was already twilight.

The sun was gone, and remnants of the snow from the night before were beginning to freeze. At first, a mistlike drift of snow began falling, then flakes light at first and heavier later, thicker and covering the ground quickly. Inside my shoes, my bare feet felt numb, and a cold wind beat against my naked calves. With head bent and hands inside the sleeves of my green jacket, crossed over my chest, I hurried along, picking up my head every once in a while to see where I was. I had to go around Dabrowa before continuing on the long track to Tarnów.

Where would I sleep? Should I keep walking all night? I

wondered. Thinking of the immensity of the project, I almost abandoned it, opting instead for safe shelter from the wind in a nearby wood, knowing full well that there was nothing else I could do for the long term. A brief rest then, and I continued to plod ahead.

In the distance I noticed a white hut that in the evening light looked blue. In its window, a light beckoned, and my heart skipped a beat. I knew that hut well. It was the home of Wladyslaw and his wife, the middle-aged couple with whom I had spent a few weeks during the summer as a shepherdess. What a long time ago that seemed, yet it could not have been more than a few months ago. I decided to ask them for shelter for the night.

What a happy welcome I got. How glad they were to see me. How warm and cozy was the clean, fragrant room. The wife, Maryna, put her arms around me and said, "You must be cold without stockings." Tears immediately welled up in my eyes.

"I am not very cold," I said as she put a bowl of hot millet with milk on the table. I ate with gusto, despite having eaten not too long ago, and when I finished eating, she brought a lice comb and spread a large sheet of paper on the floor. Handing me the comb, she instructed how to go about combing my hair onto the paper. I ran the comb through my long hair until the paper looked as if it would walk away by itself. Then I carefully crumpled it into a ball, making sure that nothing escaped, and dropped it into the fire. I felt gloriously clean after that, my scalp tingling from the workout.

For a little while longer, we sat near the hearth as I told them about all that had happened and what I planned to do in the morning. They approved of my plan, but they would not think of letting me walk that distance. The farmer would take me there in his wagon, and his wife would go along too so that it would look as if my parents were taking me because I had their approval to leave.

I did not expect to be treated with such consideration, such care. That evening I experienced some of the greatest happiness of my young life. And when they both walked me to the barn, which was now full of the square bales of hay for the winter, and spread a woolen blanket all the way near the roof, having had to climb there, I could contain myself no longer—uncontrollable tears began to flow down my cheeks. I bid them a wordless goodnight, and lying in my warm nest, I wept for as long as the tears would come.

It was still dark outside when I awoke. I heard Wladyslaw harnessing the horse to the wagon. I quickly got to my feet, folded the blanket, put on the skirt I had taken off because Maryna had pressed it the evening before, and went into the house. They had already eaten, and my breakfast was waiting on the table.

We left before there was any movement on the neighboring farms, and by the time we clattered across the cobblestones of the market in Dabrowa, an overcast day was dawning. We sat close together on the front board, keeping each other warm: the farmer in his jerkin and hat; the farmer's wife in a plaid wrap, a dark scarf with a red rose pattern tied over her head; and I in the middle in my green, light wool suit, Mother's scarf covering my hair. It was November, and a succession of gray, overcast days, accompanied by frozen rain or snow, would now herald the beginning of the long Polish winter.

I looked around the deserted town from my perch on the wagon, its ghosts staring back at me, and I momentarily lost the courage to go through with my plan. This is where I belong, I thought. Why am I running away? I was born here. I should have stayed in the transport. I would now be with Grandmother. But the wagon kept moving. We did not speak, each thinking his own thoughts, and before I could dwell on my wretched circumstances for any length of time, we were again on the open road, heading for Tarnów.

Eventually my thoughts became wholly preoccupied with the anticipated change my life would take. I wondered what it would be like to not be afraid anymore. Or would I still be afraid, this time of being discovered in Germany?

My imagination wandered to having my own room, a clean bed, for which my body ached, and food on a regular basis. I saw a white painted room with a white bed, such as I had in Katowice. The room had a window and a bookshelf with books. Those were the thoughts I was thinking now. I wanted to live. I kept thinking, I am too young to die, that same phrase I had repeated while marching in the transport from Pacanow to Szczucin. I am too young to die. I haven't lived yet. And I gave no thought to what I would have to do to earn the things of which I dreamed—a room, a bed, books.

The farmer's wife interrupted my reverie when she told me what would happen when we reached Tarnów. They would take me directly to the Arbeitsamt, let me off in front of it, and I was to enter without lingering, without hesitation. I would then register for work in Germany.

It was about nine o'clock when we reached our destination. Thanking them and hugging each with particular warmth, I walked resolutely into the Arbeitsamt, strengthened by the encouragement and care I had gotten from these two good people and by the goal that stretched before me—a promise of life after a long, dark void. I was now ready and eager to fulfill my plan. Of course, anxiety and hesitation still gnawed at me, and I knew I had to forge ahead before I lost the nerve to do what I had to do. As I opened the door to that office, I forced myself to think of my new name and the fact that I was sixteen years old.

Twenty-one

I was the first client there. Some of the clerks were dusting their desks. Others were joking with each other. I went up to one of them, a man, perhaps in his middle twenties, and told him that I wanted to register for work in Germany. He gave me an incredulous look and lazily reached for a pen and a pad of application forms.

"Your name?" He asked.

"Eva Stanek," I answered loud and clear.

"Your religion?"

"Catholic."

"Date of birth?"

"December 11, 1926." I remembered the slip of paper the farmer had given me with his daughter's birth date written on it.

"Your mother's name?" His calm voice went on as he kept filling out the form.

I felt color coming over my face. I had not thought of this kind of information and was caught unawares, but to keep up the flow, I simply gave the first name that came to mind: "Maria Stanek," I said.

"Her maiden name."

"I don't know." I was beginning to lose confidence. I had no idea how far he would probe into my family history, and I realized how unprepared I was.

He repeated the same questions for "your father's name, etc.," and I ad-libbed, making it up as I went along. I was desperate, and I gambled. I knew I would not remember all I told him should I be

219

questioned again about these things, and I sent out fervent prayers to God that this would not happen. He also wanted to know the reason for my volunteering for work in Germany, another question for which I was unprepared. I said that the work on the farm was now finished for the season and that there was nothing to do at home in winter. Another incredulous look from him, and it flashed through my mind that he might suspect me of not being the person I claimed to be. But he put all information down on the application just as I gave it to him and motioned to a chair, where I was to wait until called. I was now officially Eva Stanek, farmer's daughter, and anxious to distance myself as quickly as possible from my former identity, I felt a curious relief.

I waited until midmorning, when the door opened and in walked two policemen leading three young men and a teenage girl. From the conversation that passed between the policemen and the clerk, I gathered that these young people had been caught off the street to be sent for forced labor in Germany, the same kind of labor for which I had volunteered. They were asked the same questions I was asked, except the last one, and were later told to wait where I waited while the two policemen stationed themselves outside the entrance of the Arbeitsamt.

One of the young men sat down next to me and started a conversation. He wanted to know if I was also going to Germany, and when I said that I was, he took it for granted that I, too, had been caught against my will. I was pleased that he thought that, because that somehow reinforced my new identity, and I felt safer being part of a group.

When the clerk finally came to inform us that we would start for Krakow in the evening and that we would then be given food, my friend unpacked a piece of sausage and offered me a bite. I looked at him for a moment, hesitating, but he smiled and thrust his hand forward, encouraging me to take a piece. I took the sausage and bit into it with such enthusiasm that I bit nearly half of it off. When I handed it back, embarrassed, he looked at it for a moment, and we both laughed, I with one hand covering my full mouth. The piece of sausage I had in my mouth was too big to chew, and I struggled with it. In that time, he had eaten most of his share, but when he got to the last bite, he handed it back to me, and I ate that too.

It was turning dark outside when trucks picked us up to be transported to the railroad station. There a train waited, full of young people being taken to Krakow. We didn't know where the train came from, but it was obvious that youths from many different regions had been loaded on it. Some wore their regional costumes.

By 1942, the year I am describing here, Polish police were staging raids in cities, taking young people off the streets and loading them on trains, which took them to a central place from where they would be sent to Germany for work. Those caught were not allowed to go back home. They were being sent away in just the clothes on their backs.

Our group of five got an empty compartment, and I sat with the same boy, Jaś, because it gave me a sense of protection. But at the same time I felt uncomfortable with the idea of having a "boyfriend." I hoped that somehow this would soon resolve itself.

On the train we were each given a slice of bread with honey and ordered to eat while the train remained in the station. Later, when the train was moving, my friend and I talked of farming. I think that was all he knew. I knew very little about it, but I had told him that I came from a farm, so I had to keep up the pretense. I spoke about cows and horses and the pastures and whatever else I had recently learned.

When we exhausted that subject, he wanted to know my name and age. I told him I was sixteen. "Just right," he exclaimed happily. "I am nineteen, and you are the right age for me. And you are very pretty," he said, and I blushed. Then, "I like you." He whispered that last part into my ear so that the others, who looked as if they were sleeping, could not hear.

I took off my jacket to remove the sweater I planned to leave on the train, afraid that the insects would spread to the others if I kept it on. After that, Jaś moved closer and put his arm on the backrest of our seat. I did not know what to make of this. His behavior was more advanced than what I was used to, but I saw no harm in it. I only hoped that becoming chummy would not mean that we were going to be engaged. I was inexperienced in these matters. Although I liked his blond looks and his gentleness, I recognized that we had nothing in common, and that, after all, I was not who he thought I was.

We stopped talking for a while, but I heard his breathing, which brought back the dream I'd had while hiding out in the barn with my parents. Instinctively I moved away. He followed. To add to my discomfort, the lights on the train went out, and we remained in darkness for the rest of the trip. He began whispering in my ear, and I felt his warm breath against my skin. I did not want to make a scene, and I did not want to alienate him, so I answered in monosyllables, turning my head away, pretending to sleep. Using his free hand, he sought my chin, moved my face around to his, and feeling safe from being seen by the others in the darkness, planted a tender but burning kiss on my forehead. He held me for a moment, and I expected another assault, but suddenly the train slowed to a crawl, and we entered a busy station. The lights on the platform illuminated our compartment intermittently as we passed them, and the others, who until then had been sleeping, began to stir. When the train came to a full stop, we heard the word "Krakow" being called. The lights in the train came on, and I saw my friend's flushed face smiling at me. I straightened my hair and put the jacket over my blouse, leaving the sweater in a corner on the floor of the compartment. It was drizzling outside, and I hated to leave the warm train, but I felt relief that this strange trip was over.

Hundreds began pouring out of each open door on the train. We waited for everyone to assemble; then we were taken into an empty waiting room, guarded by grim-faced, armed soldiers. There the men were separated from the women, and while Jaś was being led away, he called out that we would meet in camp. I nodded and did not give it another thought.

From the waiting room, trucks picked us up, and it was well past midnight when we were unloaded at a huge red brick building that had possibly been a school or jail. It was now a transit camp for those going to Germany for work. Here we would spend two weeks quarantined from the outside world. Searchlights scoured the campgrounds at night, and on the inside, the building was lit with fluorescent lights day and night. The area was surrounded by a chainlink fence, topped by several rows of barbed wire. Outside the fence, all around the building marched stone-faced sentries.

There were thousands of us here, some whose waiting period was almost over, others who had recently arrived. It seemed incredible that Germany would want us all.

I realized that I was in a detention camp for the first time, though it was only a temporary situation. I did not dwell on this; instead I concentrated on what was happening around me.

In groups of thirty, we were led into dormitory rooms. In my room, the women were all in their late teens and early twenties. We each got a cot with a straw-filled sack for a mattress and a thin blanket. For me this was sheer luxury after a damp bed on pine needles. Lights were left on all night.

In the morning, after a cursory washing in a communal washroom, we were led into a large hall. In the middle of the hall stood a table set up as a desk. A small man wearing a German uniform sat behind a stack of forms. As we assembled, he shuffled papers until the hall door was closed. Then, over a loudspeaker, he announced in broken Polish that we would be counted, and we were to respond as our names were being called. After that, he would pick fifteen girls for work in German private homes and businesses. The rest would be assigned to factory work.

While he readied his papers, we were able to look around and talk. I saw Jaś, and the moment he spotted me, he came over and took my hand. I blushed but was once again glad to have this young man pay attention to me. I hoped that seeing our meeting, people would think that we came from the same village. He was a helpful part of my new identity.

We were told to quiet down, and the checking began. Jaś squeezed my hand and said, "until later," then ran back to where the men were grouped. The women from my room asked about him, and I said that he was my boyfriend. "Is he from your village?" they asked. "Yes," I smiled.

When the counting was over, the men were led away, and the women remained so that the fifteen who were to be placed in private homes and businesses could be picked. One of the women in our dorm was a tall girl of about eighteen. She had black hair and blue eyes, a bulbous nose, and a rasping voice that shifted back and forth from contralto to falsetto as she spoke. She walked with a swagger, never standing still for long. Her name was Zofie. The small man in German uniform assigned Zofie to help him choose the fifteen needed girls, or rather fourteen more because hers would be the first name on the list.

Walking among us, she looked us up and down. She passed me several times, and I hoped she would pick me, but although she stopped and looked at me, she did not choose me. When the fifteen had been picked and were standing to one side, away from the rest of us, the man looked each one over slowly. Then he walked over to his desk and looked through his files. Holding the loudspeaker close to his mouth, he called, "Eva Stanek." I came forward.

"Can you read and write?" He asked.

"Yes.

"What did you do at home?" He looked up from behind his glasses.

"I took care of the cows" came out spontaneously, and I was immediately sorry for it. A snicker rippled across the assembled women.

"But you could do other work too, couldn't you?"

"Oh yes," I answered enthusiastically. "I can do domestic work."

"Fine, step over to this group." He pointed to the group of fifteen. Thus I became the sixteenth chosen girl. I did not look at Zofie.

I could not understand, and I do not know to this day, what caused this man to look for me in particular. Had something been written on my application that caught his attention? Was it because my diction was good? But what did it matter why he picked me? I was happy that he did, and my confidence rose.

After a lunch of soup and bread, we waited for disinfection. Knowing the condition of my clothing and hair, I worried. I didn't know if finding lice on me would mean sending me back home. Disinfection, some called it delousing, turned out to be a good hot shower with lots of soap, something I was in great need of. So when the bell rang throughout the building, we assembled in the courtyard to be taken to the bathhouse.

The bathhouse had two entrances, one for women and one for men. At the entrance of the women's side was a semidark room where we were told to undress and leave our clothing. Next, we lined up for inspection. Two women inspected pubic hair and the hair on our heads. A third stood by, ready with razor in hand. Some of the girls had their hair shaved off their heads; others lost their hair on other parts of their bodies. I already began to mourn my braids. I did not care what I would look like; what worried me was the embarrassment of not being found clean. I waited my turn silently, however, and when the woman looked into my hair, I was remarkably relaxed. A moment later, I was sent to the showers—a big load off my mind.

The shower room was brightly lit, with two rows of showerheads running down its middle and a heated saunalike drying area along the walls, furnished with wooden benches. This room was separated from the men's shower room by a wall with a large window, both sides of which were hung with cotton curtains Surprised by the bright lights, I unfurled a handkerchief that I had in my hand and held it with both hands at my waist so that it covered all that part I wanted to hide. A woman attendant noticed and took my cover away.

It is almost impossible to describe today the feeling created by the warm water on my body. How long had it been since I had had a bath? I could not even remember when warm water last touched my skin. Many of the girls with whom I was bathing complained; the soap was too strong, the water too hot or not hot enough. I just stood there, letting thin, needlelike streams beat my body for as long as I was allowed to do it, and when I came out to dry, my skin was pink, and my hair hung loose and smelled fresh, giving me a feeling of well-being I had not had in years.

While we were drying, a commotion arose near the window. Some of the girls had lifted the curtain that covered the men's shower room and were flirting with the men. Everyone was, of course, naked, and I got another lesson in sex education.

During the time when we bathed, various men passed in and out of the shower room. They were presumably attendants in the bathhouse. While some girls were enjoying themselves, others were crying because they missed their families. These girls wanted to go back home, having been picked off the street against their will. Whenever one of the male attendants saw a crying girl, he would stop to talk with her, asking if she wanted to escape, and if she said yes, he would promise to assist her. A few girls organized a plot with the help of these men to run away once the disinfection was over.

Affected by the sorrowful pleadings of these girls to be able to return home, I began to cry too. I certainly did not want to stand out as a volunteer, and crying along with the others helped me to look like a good Polish daughter, I thought. On the other hand, I knew that if I was helped to escape, I would again have no place to go--it was the last thing I wanted. But I still had some fear that someone would recognize me as being Jewish, and I therefore played this dangerous game of crying in order to look authentic.

It didn't take long for a middle-aged attendant to ask if I wanted to run away. I said I missed my parents and wanted to go home. He was very sympathetic and promised to get me out of the transport legally. He could do that, he said. I had no idea what he meant by "legally," but looking at this bedraggled man, I was skeptical of his power to get me out at all, legally or otherwise. I let him go ahead with his plan because I had little choice at this point. He took a good look at me from head to toe and promised to be back shortly.

I was almost completely dry, my face no longer distorted by crying, when he returned and asked that I follow him to another room. With my left hand across my chest and my right hand covering the small area of pubic hair, I followed to where a high-ranking, overfed German officer sat on a chair too small for his corpulent body. I heard the bath attendant ask in broken German if the colonel would not be kind enough to let this girl go home, because she is so young, too young to be sent away from home.

I was still standing behind the attendant when he spoke, and the German asked him to step aside. He wanted to look at me. Taking a first look, he leaned forward and moved my hands aside.

A smile of satisfaction spread over his face. "Nein," he spoke to the attendant but kept looking at me. "Hubsches, junges madchen, gut gebaut, soll nach Deutschland gehen. Solche wollen wir. Solche brauchen wir" ("No, this young, pretty girl should go to Germany. We want her kind. We need her kind.") Unforgettable words that saved my life.

The attendant looked at me sadly as I stood expressionless, waiting for the translation, pretending not to have understood what the German said. When we walked away, the attendant told me that I would have to go on. I promptly burst into tears—not out of sorrow, as the man probably thought, but in relief. I had come close to being released again into the hell I had just escaped. But it wasn't over. Seeing me cry again, a woman attendant came over and promised to help. Dejectedly, the male attendant with whom I was walking explained that the colonel had already seen me and refused to let me go.

I thought for a long time about the life-threatening chance I had taken, allowing the attendant to help me escape from the transport. But never for a moment did I believe that this poorly dressed, broom-carrying man had the colonel's ear. Still, I had come within an inch of being released.

After that I resolved to think more carefully about what I was doing. Crying had been reckless behavior. I excused it to myself by saying that it was difficult to watch so many girls crying bitterly without breaking down also. I missed my parents too and wanted to be back with them. I felt terribly lonely and afraid, and I still believed them to be living. That was the real reason I cried in the bathhouse. Thinking that I wanted to look authentic was, I guess, just an excuse to let go. I took that terrible chance not because I was brave or clever, but because I could not control my emotions. I knew that I didn't have to cry to look authentic. After all, not all the girls cried, and not all the girls wanted to go back home.

Many were actually enjoying themselves, away from their family's watchful eyes, surrounded by hundreds of young men. It occurred to me for the first time that I might not be the only volunteer in this transport.

This incident, together with a number of others described in previous pages, remained so clear in my mind that had I never written them down, I would still have remembered each detail even after seventy years. As I think of these experiences, I see a picture so vivid, each detail so clear, that it might have happened yesterday.

The rest of my stay in that camp passed without incident, and the time flew. Each night I retired to my cot right after the evening meal, while the room was still abuzz with talk, and woke early mornings to enjoy the quietude and to think about the future, the unknown I was heading for. Sometimes I lay on my straw sack listening to the weather outside, which seemed worse with each passing day, and I was thankful for having a roof over my head and so very thankful for my life.

Here I started to keep another diary. Every morning, remembering the most significant experiences of the past few years, I wrote a single word or phrase pertaining to each experience on a scrap of paper, which I folded many times and placed in the pocket of my jacket. Those quiet early morning hours focused and strengthened me. They helped me to continue on the strange and difficult path that was my life.

I did not see much of Jaś during those days. Women took meals before the men, and our schedules were purposely staggered to keep us separated. I was relieved not to see him because I no longer felt the same need for his protection that I had felt at the beginning of that trip, and the relationship made me uncomfortable.

Our chores during the days consisted mainly of inspections: our backgrounds were checked and rechecked. We were checked again and again for cleanliness. Our clothing was cleaned and disinfected. These things helped pass the time quickly. I looked forward to leaving Krakow. As long as we remained in Poland, I felt vulnerable. Each time our home addresses were checked, our education and our birthdays, I felt there was a possibility they would detect my true identity, or if not my true identity, at least find out that I was not Eva Stanek.

Having been picked off the streets, most of the girls in the transport had no extra clothing with them, but they all had purses and other small possessions. Nobody had much baggage, but I had none. I seemed to be the only girl who owned nothing save the clothes on my back. This worried me. Although not many noticed my lack of belongings, Zofie and some of the girls whom she picked did, and they took turns asking me about this. My stock answer to their questions was, "I was picked off the street. How could I have baggage?" I resented and feared their questions, and I became distrustful of that group.

Finally the long-awaited day of departure came, and we were all up early. Since I had nothing to pack and nothing to change into, I was one of the first to be ready. Using my hands, I pressed some of the wrinkles out of my suit, washed, and went out in the hall, where people were already assembling from all corners of this huge edifice. There I saw Jaś, who, when he saw me, tried to come toward me, but he was stopped by an official. He called across the hall that he would try to make arrangements for us to travel together but was immediately told by the official that I would travel with my group in a separate car. Undaunted, he called that he would find me during our stopovers on some of the larger stations along the way. I was glad we could not travel together because I did not want another such trip as I'd had with Jaś from Tarnów to Krakow. I was glad to be spared his amorous advances.

Meanwhile the hall filled with hundreds of people talking, laughing, some crying. Roll was called for the last time, and to some of the names there was no response. Those names would be called twice more, and after that, the clerk would strike them off the list. Some time later, when roll call was over, we were told to start in pairs to the front door, where trucks waited to take us to the railroad station.

Our group of sixteen was ordered to stay together and wait until everyone else left the building. But the group of sixteen had shrunk to a group of twelve. Four had apparently made their escape.

The railroad station was that day closed to the public and was surrounded by armed soldiers, some of whom were also walking among us inside the station. Out on the track, a train waited, and with much commotion, cries for lost items, vows to stay in touch, and laughter, the train was loaded to capacity. Our group stood apart, waiting for directions. Eventually we were led by two German civilians to a first-class car with red upholstered seats and curtains on the windows. The car was not heated. At that point in the war, everyone knew there was a scarcity of fuel. Thoughts of the cold brought to mind some of my geography classes, where I had learned that Germany was warmer than Poland because it was located farther south, and I looked forward to the warmer climate. It was November 1942, and Poland was already in the throes of winter. I wondered what Germany would be like in November.

Steam hissed, someone blew a whistle, and slowly, to the accompaniment of intermittent puffs from its stack, the train moved out of the station. A watery snow was falling, covering the tracks with slush. I shivered imperceptibly as I stood at the window, watching the changing scene in cold, drab Poland, and it made me think of my recent tragedies and my wretchedness. My country—I was being expelled. And I also thought of how much happiness this country had given me, how good it was to grow in its simple, wholesome lap. To belong to those fields and forests and mountains. To experience its gentle sun in summer, and the bewitching snow in winter. What joy it was to continually discover and use in different ways its beautiful language, to sing its songs, and to act in its plays. I was leaving now, and I left behind my entire family: parents, aunts, uncles, cousins, and my beloved grandmother, all of whom will forever remain on my country's bloodstained soil. Tears coursed down my cheeks as I watched the landscape moving rapidly away from the speeding train.

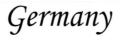

Germany

Twenty-two

With Krakow far behind, we scattered over the compartments and stretched out in comfortable seats. I kept mostly to myself. I found little in common with the other girls, who were older and more sophisticated than I. They talked about things of which I knew nothing, and when with them, I just sat listening. I kept thinking that they did not want me around. I had not forgotten that I was not Zofie's choice for her group. The two Germans who traveled with us took periodic strolls through the car, keeping check on what we were doing. Otherwise, we traveled undisturbed.

The trip took at least two days and a night. I remember the night to have been a sleepless one. I was too excited to sleep, and I spent most of it at the window. I knew by the landscape that we had left Poland behind. There was not a trace of snow anywhere. The countryside looked different too, not as starkly bare as it was in Poland at this time of year. Gleaming white huts, covered by steep brown thatch roofs, showed dark-stained wooden frameworks. They looked larger, better kept, more affluent than those in the Polish countryside, and the fields were not yet completely bare of crops.

Through the night the train stopped at various stations, but no one was allowed to get off. Once we got deeper into Germany, we stopped several times during the day, where we were told to get off the train to stretch and to get food.

On the platforms, German women were pouring ersatz coffee and handing out slices of dark bread they called Komissbrot.

We walked around eating and talking in hushed tones; none of the chaotic exuberance displayed at the station in Krakow accompanied those meals. We were now in Germany, and the mood was somber.

I thought of Jaś, but I did not see him. It didn't look as if he were trying to find me. I was sure he had a new girl by now. I never saw him again.

After the meal, we boarded the train and sometimes remained in the station for hours without moving. No explanation was given for these delays. When we finally started pulling out, throbbing voices singing sad Polish songs could be heard from the overcrowded cars in back until the train picked up speed and drowned out the singing.

Speeding into a new life, in comfort, albeit hungry, I drank in the beauty of an afternoon sun as it colored the landscape with its honey hues. Here, many trees still had not shed their leaves, and the colors added to the romantic picture. I imagined myself entering a fairy tale where everything was beautiful and cheerful, and I felt lighthearted, happy in my newly acquired safety. I began to feel the full benefit of my new identity, and I thought of how proud my parents would be if they knew that I was now in better circumstances than I had been a few weeks ago. Never for even an instant did I think that my parents might not be alive—those thoughts did not enter my mind. All the tragedies I witnessed were momentarily forgotten. I thought happy, hopeful thoughts. I envisioned a future, whereas I could not have done so two or three weeks ago. I conjured up dreams of a room that was clean and warm and that belonged to me. I pictured myself belonging to a library where I could read after work. I even imagined having a radio so I could listen to music. I hoped I could somehow continue to go to school. My German was good, and language would not be a barrier. I only pretended in the transport not to understand it.

Of course, my imagination was running wild because I had not the vaguest notion of what I would and what I would not be able to do or even what my life would be like in Germany. Sitting at the window and watching the rapidly changing landscape, I continued to daydream while looking at a country so beautiful that, enchanted, I whispered over and over, "Bajka" (fairytale in Polish).

The girls visited each other and teased me for sitting alone so much of the time, but I did not want to talk. I didn't want to dispel the good feelings of comfort I was enjoying.

We were not told that Stuttgart would be our destination. But it did not matter—one place would do as well as another. When we arrived in Stuttgart, we were separated from the rest of the transport, and with a police escort, the twelve of us were led to an empty bus, which took us to the Arbeitsamt, where prospective employers were already waiting.

I was quickly assigned to a fiery-looking, red-haired Teuton who owned a restaurant, and as we were leaving the Arbeitsamt, I heard Zofie call my name. She ran up to me, and giving my employer a beatific smile, she asked what my new address would be. To me she said in Polish that I was lucky to be assigned to a restaurant—I would have plenty to eat. She hoped for a similar position.

After writing down her address for Zofie, my lady employer quickly whisked me out of the Arbeitsamt. She seemed in a hurry, and I got my first "mach schnell" (hurry up) from her.

The restaurant was actually a small inn with a few guest rooms and a tavern. It was referred to as the Brauhouse. The dining room was mahogany paneled; its windows were stained glass. Never having been inside a tavern, I thought it handsome, and I liked it immediately. I also liked the white and stainless steel kitchen where I would spend most of my time, and I liked the private part of the house where, in an upper storey, I shared a room with the general maid. It was all cheerful and inviting and incredibly clean.

As I was soon to find out to my regret, I rarely had the time to enjoy my new home.

The Brauhouse was situated just outside the city of Stuttgart. I believe it was in Ditzingen, but I am not sure of the town's name because I did not write it down. The suburb was quiet and respectable. My employers seemed like decent people, very German in their characteristics: clean beyond anything imaginable, frugal, efficient, demanding.

Constant demands were made on me, demands that had to be executed without delay. "Mach schnell" accompanied every order, and excuses were not acceptable. My pay was room and board, and I was to get 25 deutsche mark at the end of each month. Food and bed were all I really wanted, so the money I was promised did not mean a lot to me. Since there was no merchandise in the stores, and everything (food, clothing, and all other staples) went by ration cards, which none of us workers saw because our employers kept them for us, there was not much one could buy with the money anyway.

Five people worked in the Brauhouse: the two owners, the waitress, a maid, and I. The woman owner was the cook, and her husband was bartender and host. I was the kitchen maid, and the waitress helped clean and shine the kitchen before going home for the night. The maid cleaned the house, including the guest rooms. I shared a room with her, but we rarely talked because I was usually in bed and fast asleep by the time she came up after a day's work. My days were exhausting, and the only pleasure to which I could look forward was falling into that comfortable bed with its big square down pillows.

My employers burned the clothes in which I arrived, and I was given some skirts, blouses, underwear, and nightclothes from their twelve-year-old daughter, who lived in the country with her grandparents for the duration of the war. They were surprised that a sixteen-year-old girl could fit into a twelve-year-old's clothes.

Before my clothes were to be burned, I took out of my suit pockets the folded pieces of paper.

"Why are you savings these scraps of paper?" I was asked.

"Because they are notes from friends and addresses from people at home." I could not say that I kept a diary. This might have aroused suspicion. Keeping a diary in Poland in those days was quite common for a girl from a middle-class home. But keeping an eloquent diary in Germany while doing maid's work was not only incongruous, it was dangerous. It would have meant taking a serious risk of being discovered.

I had learned something very important by taking the chance of crying in the bathhouse in Krakow, that I was playing with fire and that I could not give free rein to my emotions if I wanted to stay alive. After that incident, I had promised myself to carefully consider what I was doing. And that was what I remembered when I wrote my diary in Germany, using those single words as a kind of code. Reading my notes, no one could have easily pieced together my past, nor even determine what the notes were about. Doing it that way also kept the volume down, and when at the end of the war I transcribed all words into sentences, the total came to twelve sheets of paper, each sentence lifting a curtain on the experience it described. After a week in Germany, I still could not fully grasp the change. I often got lost in a dreamlike trance, which I tried to hide from my employers. My work was not satisfactory. I was being shifted from dishwashing to the cleaning of vegetables and finally to the cleaning of the restaurant dining room. I had no idea how to do the kind of work required of me.

In front of the kitchen sink, I stood for hours washing stacks of plates thoroughly on both sides before putting them in rinse water, but that was going too slow, and on busy evenings, they would have to wait for my clean plates before the orders from the dining room could be filled.

I had never heard of washing potatoes before they were peeled, and I had never seen potatoes boiled in their jackets. In Germany, nobody peeled potatoes before boiling because too much was wasted that way. So when I was given a sack of potatoes to wash, I used the point of a knife to scoop out the eyes and then simply used my hands to swish them around a bit in a sink full of water. This was such an elementary task for the people with whom I worked that they did not even show me the brush with which such things were done, expecting me to know. I also did not get any better with the mopping of the large Brauhouse floor. All these things were making me unhappy, and despite the comfortable bed and fresh clothing I was given, I worried because I did not know what my inability to do the job would lead my employers to do with me.

I had another worry. I was not getting enough food, or perhaps not the right food. The three limited meals a day did not satisfy me. I worked long hours, expending physical energy on tasks that also drained me emotionally. My day started at six in the morning and ended at ten at night, with only an hour or so off in the afternoon, when I usually took care of personal needs, such as hand laundry and so forth. I was always hungry, but everyone in Germany lived on ration cards, even those of us who worked in restaurants. One of the things I remember about ration cards was that each individual received one fresh egg per month. To supplement my inadequate meals, therefore, I began to take food when no one was around to see it, and since I had not had meat in a very long time, and because my meals contained only miniscule portions of meat, if any, I began with an occasional slice of sausage, hoping it would go unnoticed.

With the passage of time, I learned what was expected of me, and I was becoming good at what I did. At first I had some difficulty understanding what people were saying because their Swabian dialect was so different from the pure German I knew, but in due course, I learned to speak Schwabish and, with the waitress's help, began to understand even what some of the customers were saying. Soon this lady allowed me, on slow nights, to take some of the plates to the tables, where to my delight the customers thanked me and sometimes even engaged me in conversation.

My job took on organization: I washed dishes, scrubbed vegetables, carried full plates to the window, where the waitress picked them up, and kept the kitchen clean. The owners began to smile at me.

I stopped worrying, but I was lonely. I wanted to go to Stuttgart, where I had parted with the rest of the transport. I couldn't. I got only a few hours off every other Sunday afternoon, and I was afraid that I would not be able to get back in time to help with the cold supper that was served at the Brauhouse Sunday evenings. I also did not know where any of the other girls had been placed, nor did I know how to travel to Stuttgart. But all that was not what held me back. What held me from venturing out was that I did not really know whom I wanted to see. I hadn't formed any close attachment with any of the girls with whom I had traveled to Germany. So I spent Sunday afternoons in my room, alone because the maid with whom I shared the room went home on Sundays.

I took baths. I changed into clean clothes. I spent hours sitting at the window, resting and watching the empty, cold street until my name was called in the kitchen, which meant that it was time to ready the plates with cold cuts for customers who would soon be arriving for supper.

I was in Germany about four, perhaps six, weeks when after a day's work, I was preparing for bed but was stopped by the sound of howling sirens, a frightening sound I had not heard before. I rushed back down where everyone was crowding into the basement, urging me to come along quickly. This was an air raid. From everyone's hushed conversation, I gathered that Stuttgart had never been bombed before. No one spoke to me. I was the enemy.

Was I the cause of this alarm, as it was called? I did not understand their attitude. I was as frightened as everyone else. Suddenly a tremendous explosion nearby rocked our building, and we moved farther down the basement steps. Then more explosions, but these were farther away. Everyone looked frightened and upset.

A while later, the sounding sirens announced the end of the alarm, and we went upstairs and out on the street. The sky was lit by fires that burned in many places—Stuttgart was aflame, but no bomb had fallen in our vicinity. Many bad and threatening comments were made against "those bad Tommies" by the people with whom I stood watching. When we finally went back into the house, I went upstairs at once, and before falling asleep, I thought that here at least one saw war, not just the slaughter of unarmed, innocent thousands such as I had witnessed in Poland. Yes, this was war. I slept well that night and had difficulty waking up for work the next morning.

Neither my employers nor anyone else in the restaurant behaved in the same kindly manner toward me after those first bombs fell on Stuttgart. They were not used to being attacked and were highly resentful of it. I felt their hostility and my isolation acutely.

Without consideration of the consequences, I now started taking raw frankfurters and eating them in the upstairs bathroom. It didn't take long for my woman employer to call me into the bathroom one evening and show me the skin of a frank that I had thrown into the bowl and forgotten to flush.

"Did you do this?" she asked, knowing full well that no one else would have done it.

"Yes," I answered simply. She sent me back to my room without a word.

The next day I was told to pack my things, and she brought me back to the Arbeitsamt in Stuttgart. There she told the clerk that she was bringing me back because I was not able to do the heavy work in a restaurant.

Twenty-three

My wait at the Arbeitsamt was not long. The clerk made a call, and within minutes, a tall woman with flashing brown eyes entered.

"Guten Tag, Frau Kipp," the clerk called out to her.

"Guten Tag, woh ist sie?" (where is she?) she responded. "Oh, what a little thing she is," she exclaimed when I was pointed out to her. "But she'll do fine, fur die Kinder." (for the children)

To me it seemed that I had shrunk a little standing beneath her and looking up at her formidable frame. By the time she ushered me out of the office, I felt like a dwarf. Pushing me gently ahead of her and smirking mockingly, she guided me, with my bundle of clothes, toward Bismark Strasse, where the Kipps owned a bakery and coffeehouse—it was the right place for a starved orphan. Unlike anywhere else in Germany, here bread was plentiful, and there was cake too.

The household consisted of Mr. and Mrs. Kipp, their two children, Manfred and Gisela, ages five and seven; Selma, a pure German, their kinderfraulein (whose place I was to take while she was promoted to family cook); and Bonnie, a stocky middle-aged woman who adored Mr. Kipp and who worked hand-in-hand with him baking bread and pastries for the bake shop and the coffeehouse. Lillie, the saleslady in the bake shop, and two waitresses in the coffeehouse where not included in the family because they went home after work while the rest of us resided in the apartment building where the Kipps had their business.

Seven women worked with just one man. All able-bodied men were away fighting in the war. Herr Kipp was exempted from the draft because of an injury he claimed but that was not visible and did not seem to handicap him.

From the start, it did not look as if I would be able to handle the children. My problems were such as only a thirteen-year-old could have with two spoiled brats. They did not listen to me, made fun of my German, and spoke such a heavy Schwabian dialect that I misunderstood much of what they said. That, of course, was more reason for laughter, and I was being ridiculed constantly. When for the first time Selma asked me to give the children their lunch, in my confusion and anger caused by their derision, I misunderstood her, and instead of feeding the children, I promptly helped myself to the mashed potatoes and chicken prepared by her for Manfred and Gisela. Frau Kipp was not amused.

Observing my struggle, Herr Kipp suggested I come to the bakery to help him and Bonnie; another girl would be looked for to cook for the family while Selma was reinstated as kinderfraulein. It was not difficult to find help because of the transports of people constantly arriving for labor from countries occupied by Germany. Help was not only easy to get, it was also very cheap. And so a French woman joined our staff to do the cooking and to take general charge of the kitchen.

Francoise was another stocky middle-aged woman, but unlike Bonnie, who was self-assured and bossy, Francoise was so shy that she never made eye contact with anyone. She kept the kitchen spotless and after work, disappeared to her room, which she constantly decorated and redecorated with odd swatches of material.

At the Kipps I got an attic room on the fifth floor of the apartment building. It was actually a tiny two-room apartment, but I was allowed only one of the rooms. I took the one in front, with its large mahogany, marble-topped bureau and the white iron bed that stood in an alcove. The window on the slanted ceiling opened to face a church steeple across the street. On Sundays, the peal of church bells would let me know that I could remain in bed later than my usual 5 a.m. The two rooms (really just cubicles) were connected by an open arch.

Down the hall, Selma had her room, and across the hall lived Gaston, a Dutchman who was renting his room from the owners of the building. Francoise, the new cook, had another of the cubbyholes in the attic, where she kept to herself, rarely venturing out after work. But the three of us, Gaston, Selma, and I, spent an occasional hour together after work, talking and laughing. Eventually, Selma and I became good friends. We spent evenings together talking and going to the movies on Sundays. She was eighteen years old, sandy haired, with the unusual combination of one blue eye and one brown.

Selma worked at the Kipps' to fulfill her Pflightyahr. The Pflightyahr law was passed in Germany so that all young women, regardless of background, would serve their country in whatever capacity they were called upon. The word means a year of compulsory service.

Gaston was a recent Folksdeutche convert, working at a regular well-paying job, but he could not serve in the military because he was a Dutch citizen. As an independent tenant in the building, he did not know the Kipps.

Bonnie's room was on the ground floor of the building because she often fired the bakery ovens throughout the night and had to be near them. She was a woman in middle age who considered all young girls silly geese. She only spoke with Herr and Frau Kipp or when she ordered us young ones around.

Selma did not like the Kipps, but she enjoyed the children. She disliked Frau Kipp for her short temper and her superior attitude toward the help, and she did not like Herr Kipp's familiar manner with her. Selma was engaged to a young soldier who was away at war.

Work at the bakery required strength and endurance, but the real hardship was having to start the day at dawn. My work included sifting flour in large hand-operated sieves, firing the furnace, fetching butter from the cellar for baking, and carrying boards loaded with loaves of bread up a dark stairway from the bakery to the bake shop. At moments when I was unobserved going upstairs, I played with a tiny mouse whom I had made a pet. Unfortunately, Herr Kipp soon discovered that relationship and stood by while he forced me to kill my little pet by stepping on her when he trapped her in a corner. "A mouse in a bakery can cause untold damage! I am surprised and disappointed that you did not know this," he yelled.

Ordinarily, Herr Kipp was a warm, easygoing man who treated me with consideration. Bonnie tolerated me because Herr Kipp did, and she would have done anything to please him.

The very best part of working in the bakery was not having anything to do with Frau Kipp. I dreaded her temper, which she displayed at the slightest provocation.

For the big meal of the day, which we ate at noon, both Kipps and the staff gathered in the large kitchen that adjoined the bakery. That was the only time in the day I saw Frau Kipp. She rarely came down from the coffeehouse, where she cashiered. Immediately after dinner, Herr Kipp took a nap in a little study off the bake shop, and there too he and Frau Kipp took their evening meals, away from everyone.

With the exception of air raids, which were now occurring with greater frequency, there were no surprises in my days. I worked long hours and filled what was left of my time with everyday trivialities, such as cleaning my room or washing my hair. I rose at dawn to work until evening, when, exhausted, I could hardly wait to go to sleep. When I wasn't tired, I spent time with Selma or Gaston.

I lived without any kind of real news of the world. I was aware only of my immediate surroundings, and not even fully of those. Reports given on the radio and in the newspapers were mostly of Germany's annihilation of the rest of Europe. I didn't know whether or not to believe this. I could not ask anyone, but I listened to conversations. To show interest was suspect.

Selma

From our dinner conversations, at which Frau Kipp held center stage, I found out that the Germans were now using a missile, or flying bomb, called V2, which was being discharged in Germany, pointed at London, England. London suffered great losses because of these long-range missiles, and I remember Frau Kipp being especially excited and pleased about this. She only

Gaston

wished these flying bombs could be directed at New York. Herr Kipp never joined this kind of talk. It is difficult to say if he feared future reprisals for those sentiments from the foreigners sitting at his table, or if he did not share his wife's feelings.

Before too many bombs fell on Stuttgart, I sometimes took Sunday afternoon walks and found the city I lived in to be clean and beautiful. Handsome buildings and wide streets stretched for miles, strewn with old churches, galleries, movie and coffeehouses where, for a few stamps from one's ration card, one could get a slice of torte and coffee. I could not buy these things because my employers held my ration card.

Time was passing, and I was already a well-established member of the Kipp household when, on a certain day, while walking up the dark stairway, a wooden board loaded with loaves of bread sitting on my shoulder, I heard my name whispered in Polish. When I looked up, I saw Zofie standing before me. She had gone to visit me at the Brauhouse, and they had told her to call the Arbeitsamt, where she got my present address. I was completely surprised by her visit. I now rarely thought of her and the other girls, and Zofie was not a particular favorite with me because I could not forgive her for not choosing me for special work in Krakow. But there she stood, her manner urgent, her face lit up in a smile. She was thinner than I remembered her, and her clothing was stylish. I told her to go down to the bakery and wait for me. I had to unload the bread in the shop.

Later, after introducing Zofie to Herr Kipp and Bonnie, I was able to sit on the stairs for a few minutes of talk. She told me that five of the girls from our group had been detached by the Arbeitsamt after our arrival in Stuttgart and sent to factory work instead of the private work for which they had been selected. Zofie had been placed in a restaurant of poor quality in a declining neighborhood, and the other three, Anna, Maria, and Jean, had been sent to work in a tuberculosis sanatorium in Heilbronn. This left two girls with whom she was unable to make contact.

It appeared that her visit had multiple purposes. She asked if I could, once in a while, bring some bread and perhaps some other food to the girls who worked in the factory, and she gave me their address. I promised I would try. I also took the address of the girls at the tuberculosis sanatorium in Heilbronn because I wanted to write to them.

To this point I had never left the Kipp household for any extended trip beyond city limits. Having had to wear a yellow *P* to identify me as a Pole, I could not go to the cinema or any other places of entertainment. I assumed that the same would apply to traveling. Finally, Herr Kip told me to remove the *P* from my wardrobe and never wear it again. He said I looked so much like a German girl that no one would suspect me of being anything but German. After I removed the *P* from my clothes, I went to the movies some Sundays. It gave me a place to spend some of my earned money and to enjoy an afternoon.

Now, while still talking with Zofie, I already began making mental plans to visit the factory and bring bread to those girls from our group who had not been fortunate enough to have been placed in private employment. I even planned to take the train to Heilbronn on my next holiday.

I could tell that Zofie was impressed with my job and my boss. She commented on all the breads and cakes that stood around in abundance, and she blushed with pleasure when Herr Kipp engaged her in polite conversation. She asked to see my room, and I asked Herr Kipp for permission to spend a little more time with my friend. We walked up the five flights to my cubbyhole, and feeling freer there, she at once asked me to do her a favor. She had a sister in Poland who, she said, was in some kind of trouble with a boyfriend and could I help arrange for Herr Kipp to ask the authorities for her services. I instantly promised to help, and I assured her that, in fact, the Kipps were looking for more help. But I was puzzled. "Why," I asked, "do you want her to come to Germany when you yourself were so unhappy to have been caught for this work?" Her face reddened, and she gave no answer. "Why do you want your sister to come here to work so hard?" I persisted.

"You see," she finally stammered. "We are orphans, and no one in Poland cares what happens to her. I am her only relative, and we want to be together." She looked at me appealingly and it briefly crossed my mind how the tables had turned. The self-assured Zofie was seeking my help. Where was that bravado with which she had stridden around camp in Krakow?

"Let's go see Herr Kipp right now and we can talk with him together," I said. But she didn't move. She remained standing and looked at me for a while as if she were making up her mind about something. Then out of the blue she said, "Aren't you Jewish?" I sat down on my bed, thinking my legs would not hold me up, and pointed to the only chair in the room. It had been months since I had heard or even thought the word "Jewish." In fact, my being Jewish occupied my mind less and less; I willed it so, because I wanted to be what I pretended to be to ease the burden that weighed on me. I wanted no complications. I wished my life to be simply that which it appeared to be. Hearing the word that could mean death stunned me. It was as if a thunderbolt had hit unexpectedly. Zofie's whispered words were reaching me again. "You can tell me," she said. After a moment of looking straight into her eyes, I said, "Why?"

"Why what?" She asked.

"Why do you ask, and why can I tell you?" My eyes did not leave hers. So we sat for what seemed like an eternity. Then she dropped her bag on the floor and, still holding my gaze, said in a barely audible whisper, "Because I am Jewish, and Anna is Jewish, and Maria and Jean, we are all Jewish. We admitted it to each other when we were still in Poland."

I was flabbergasted, and the heaviness her question had brought on lifted off me at once. Grinning, with tears coursing down my face, I told her that I too was Jewish, and we hugged.

For the rest of that day and way into the night, I thought of nothing but how Zofie and I had acknowledged our identities to each other and what happiness it was to know that I had some friends whose background was similar to mine, from whom I need hide nothing. I wondered why I had not suspected her of being Jewish when her face (now that I thought of it) betrayed her Semitic roots. When I had come out of the woods, after weeks of solitude, hunger, and fear, I had lost perspective. It had never occurred to me that other Jewish girls and young women may be saving themselves in the same way as I.

During those first days in Germany, when I had begun to realize that I might actually survive the war, I had thought I was the only Jewess to have come to Germany. And I had thought how wonderful it was that farmer Stanek had a daughter whom I could impersonate. I thought my case was singular. Finding others of my faith in the middle of Germany—in pure, Aryan, Judenfrei Third Reich—during the Second World War, which Germany at that time was still winning, was extraordinarily thrilling and extraordinarily frightening.

Zofie and I did not ask each other our real names; I guess we did not think of it. We knew that we all lived under assumed names, and even after the war, we (all the girls in our particular group) kept those first names from the war years, taking back only our surnames when the war ended.

When Zofie and I finally came back down to the bakery, Herr Kipp was pleased that someone would want to come from Poland, especially to his establishment, and after Zofie produced a postcard-size photograph of her beautiful sister, he was even more pleased and flattered. All I knew of Zofie's sister was that her name was Maria and that she was twenty-one years old.

Herr Kipp started work on Maria's arrival in Germany, and

although I was not told any of the details, in a very short time, he announced that Maria would arrive in about three months, as papers were being prepared for her arrival by the Arbeitsamt in Stuttgart.

Zofie now became a regular visitor at Kipp bakery. On her half day off from work she would come, ostensibly to inquire about the progress of her sister's working papers; but having been assured by Herr Kipp and by letter from her sister that all was progressing according to plan, her visits had another purpose: while walking up the dark stairs to the shop level, I would slip a loaf of bread into her large bag and sometimes even one of the génoise rounds that were cooling on racks along with the loaves of bread before being frosted into layer cakes. She was always grateful for this help.

On Sundays I now visited the five girls who had been part of our special group when we left Krakow. They worked in a munitions factory outside Stuttgart. There I carried bread and, occasionally, whenever I thought I could take some without it being missed, a quarter-pound package of butter. Little, if any, fat was allotted foreign workers, and the butter I brought was greatly valued. Once, Francoise saw me take the butter. She looked me full in the face without saying anything, then winked when I stammered out my reason for taking it.

During one of the visits to the factory barracks, I met Reno, a tall, handsome Pole around twenty years old. I could not keep my eyes off him, although we rarely spoke. He eventually started walking me back to the bus stop when I was ready to return home. But he tired of this routine quickly. He was so much older and more serious than I. An intellectual, he found me uninteresting. I strained to be older, more sedate, but he could not put up with the affectation. I felt this rejection deeply, and I was embarrassed by it, angry at myself for not being able to keep his interest. I thought of stopping my visits to the barracks, but I didn't. My near total lack of social life caused me to go back. I liked being with Polish-speaking people who sang Polish songs and displayed friendly good humor. So I continued my visits, although not with the same enthusiasm as before—that is, not until Henry came into the picture.

Henry was one of the boys who attended our Sunday gatherings. He had always been there, but compared to Reno, he was insignificant. He also paid no attention to me, which intensified his insignificance. At seventeen, he looked for a woman older than himself. Dark, wiry, fast, he flitted from one pretty girl to another in quick succession.

Intrigued by his behavior, I began to make myself attractive for him. Without telling me about it, the girls whom I visited noted my new interest and, wanting to help me get over Reno, tried to persuade Henry to walk me to the bus Sunday evenings. Weeks later, he asked if I wanted him to walk me. When the bus came, I was surprised to see him board it instead of returning to the barracks. He would take me all the way home, he said.

It was a trip I will never forget. He played games I did not understand and for which I was unprepared. Looking at me from under his long dark lashes, he said things that confused and embarrassed me. I answered by smiling coyly and lowering my eyelids as I tried to keep up my part of the game. He took my hand, and I felt warm and slightly damp all over. He was still holding my hand when the bus pulled in at the depot in Stuttgart, and he did not let go of it until we reached the front entrance of the building I lived in. There he pushed me against the heavy wrought iron entrance door and deftly wrapped both his arms around me, pressing his large wet mouth against my tightly closed lips. My lips remained pressed together while he maneuvered his tongue around them. I tried to figure out what to do, but I took too long. Tired of trying, he finally let go, looked at me for an instant, and said, "Next time will be better." With that, he turned away and disappeared into the darkness.

He never joined the Sunday gatherings at the barracks after that. As for me, I often thought about that evening and his kiss.

Twenty-four

During one afternoon break, when Selma and I were in our rooms doing personal chores, I was surprised to find red stains on my underwear. I ran to Selma for counsel. When I told her what I had seen, she smiled and confirmed my suspicion—I had gotten my period. She said, "Let's go see Frau Kipp."

After Frau Kipp heard what Selma told her, she asked her to handle the cash register, then told me to come along to Herr Kipp's little study. There she explained how to take care of myself and handed me a box of sanitary napkins and a belt, showing me how they worked. When she was sure that I understood her instructions, she offered a few admonishing words not to allow boys to get fresh with me. I was now grown up, and I was not to act silly or foolish, but with restraint as became a young lady. This said, she left me to ponder my new stage in life.

On a busy morning while Bonnie, Herr Kipp, and I were baking, we heard the sound of boots and the clink of spurs on the stairway leading down to the bakery. A ruddy-faced policeman walked in smiling.

"Morgen," he called out, addressing himself to Herr Kipp, who, dressed in white, looked up from the kneading board. "What can I do for you?"

"You have an employee here by the name of Eva Stanek?"

"Yes," the smile which nearly always hovered around Herr Kipp's face vanished.

"Is she a good employee?" The policeman was still smiling.

"Yes, a very good employee."

"Das Dritte Reich has an offer for Miss Stanek. We wish her to become a Folksdeutsche. Her identification papers and her photos mark her as a candidate of purity. Good coloring, excellent behavior, young, with good intelligence." He took on an air of importance, his eyes searching mine for a reaction as he obviously recognized me as the person he was looking for, but I just stood grinning foolishly because I could think of nothing else to do.

Bonnie's floured face, mouth slightly open, eyes smiling, looked on speechless. Herr Kipp seemed to me on the verge of laughter, but he did not laugh.

"Give her some time to think about this. She will contact you after she has made her decision," he said, looking straight at the policeman, whose ruddy face no longer smiled.

"I am surprised to hear you say that, Herr Kipp. Is this not the greatest honor we can bestow on a foreigner? Offering her a chance to become a German national?" The policeman held Herr Kipp's gaze.

"Yes, of course, without question, but you must understand my point of view. The girl is in some way my responsibility, and she hardly understands the situation," said Herr Kipp with finality. Then he shot Bonnie a meaningful look and asked her to wrap a nice fresh loaf of bread for the officer, not giving anyone a chance to say anything else.

While Bonnie busied herself wrapping the bread, I braved a "danke schoen," which the policeman acknowledged with a salute. Then he took the bread from Bonnie, raised his right hand high, and called out "Heil Hitler" as he ran up the dark stairway.

When the sound of the departing policeman could no longer be heard, Herr Kipp motioned me to follow him to the private study that was the Kipps' sanctuary.

"Did you understand what the policeman said?" He asked.

"Yes, it was very clear." I was about to smile, but seeing his serious face, I didn't.

He then told me not to even entertain the thought of becoming a Folksdeutsche. The war, he said, was now not going well for the Germans, and this was not the time to want to be German. "If, however, things turn around in our favor," he pointed to himself, "then you might want to think about this offer."

It was then the end of 1943, and the war had, indeed, turned in the Allies' favor.

I looked at this man, whose dark hair and face were dusted with flour, his white apron tied around his body, and whose usually laughing eyes were so serious now, and I was shocked. I was shocked at what he had said to the policeman, and I was even more shocked at what he said to me. The man was supposed to be my archenemy. Would he have protected me in the same way if he had known I was Jewish? I wondered.

Anxious to show my agreement to everything he suggested, I nodded, and without another word, he opened the door and we both went back down to the bakery.

That evening I wrote the following words on a piece of paper:

Policeman
Color
Young

The postman usually dropped off the mail upstairs in the bakeshop, and if there was anything for those of us who worked downstairs, Lillie, the saleslady, brought it down. But that happened rarely. The only downstairs person who sometimes got mail was Selma. In my two years at the Kipps, I got two letters, presumably from my family in Poland.

Zofie said that not getting mail from home might arouse suspicion. I did not write farmer Stanek nor anyone else in Poland fearing to reveal my whereabouts, and so I received no mail. But Zofie, eager to reciprocate for what I had done for her sister, wrote Marie, who was still in Poland, and asked her to have someone from there write me a letter. I could then pretend that it was from my parents.

I remember the first letter—one poorly handwritten page, expressing affection and sadness at my being so far away. I shed abundant tears over it in the presence of Herr Kipp and Bonnie, both of whom showed their sympathy by allowing me to take time to read and cry for as long as I needed to.

The second letter did not evoke the same reaction from me because the content was not as emotional; it was not written by the same person. But I forced myself to cry, remembering how Herr Kipp and Bonnie had respected my feelings that first time. Yet something in that second letter must have struck me as being funny because although I cried while I read it, I could not contain myself and suddenly burst out laughing and could not stop. I continued hysterical for quite some time, thinking of the tragicomedy of this performance until Bonnie, annoyed, rebuked me. "You have your tears and your laughter all in the same sack, don't you?" Herr Kipp looked at me uncomprehendingly. They liked me better when I was sad and needy.

After Marie arrived in Germany, I did not get any more mail, and I was just as glad. It was emotionally unnerving to get letters from strangers over which I had to shed tears. Besides, I didn't think it mattered to the Kipps whether I got mail or not, especially at that time, when the war was raging closer to Germany, and every German in that household was more concerned with the war than with me. Mail delivery became irregular, and after a while, it stopped altogether.

Doing laundry in our communal sink up in the attic one afternoon, I heard sobs—they came from Selma's rooms. I tiptoed over to her door and called her name softly. She let me in and continued to cry. Then, in a torrent of words, she told me how her boyfriend's mother had written her that Herman had been taken prisoner and apparently sent to America. He would not be able to write her from there, but his mother was informed that he was alive and well. Selma's worry was that with all the good food he would get in America, Herman would not want to return to Germany after the war. She wailed and considered her life to be over without him.

We talked until it was time to go back to work, and touched because I had listened to her outpourings, she invited me to spend part of Christmas day with her and her relatives in the country. I was thrilled to accept.

I told Bonnie about this invitation, who told Herr Kipp, who told Frau Kipp, and we spent a lot of time the next day at dinner talking about my trip. Everyone in the Kipp household now knew and discussed my invitation to Selma's house for Christmas dinner. But there was a problem—I literally had nothing to wear. Clothing was not to be had. The stores did not even have bare essentials, and like food, clothing was rationed. Even if it had been available in the stores, no ration card could have supplied me with all I needed. The clothes I had brought with me from my first job were too small now, and I wore them only because I had nothing else.

Francoise, the cook, said she would make me a dress if she had material. We all looked at her, surprised that she was taking part in the conversation. She rarely spoke. Seeing her interest, Herr Kipp told a funny story about a dressmaker that made as all laugh. Francoise laughed hardest, dropping her upper plate of false teeth into her bowl of soup. After that, she never spoke at dinner again.

A few days later, I was surprised by Lillie with a simple navy blue silk dress, the belt of which was decorated with an elaborate silver buckle fashioned like a clam shell. And shortly before Christmas, Frau Kipp presented me with a dark blue winter coat and hat to match.

My New Outfit

She'd had a dressmaker make them out of her old wool coat. All my new things fitted perfectly even though they were made without measuring me for them.

Those gifts left me glowing for days. They were the only well-fitting clothes I possessed until the end of the war.

When I tried on my new outfit, everyone was called to the Kipps' study to admire me, and Lillie said to Herr Kipp, "Look at your Eva now. She looks like a German girl." This was meant as a great compliment.

The awaited day came. Decked out in my new clothes, I took the bus going to Tubingen, planning to get off along the way at the address given me by Selma. She was to wait for me at the bus stop. But I got off at the wrong stop and had to walk the rest of the way, which turned out to be quite a few kilometers.

The day was beautiful, crisp, and clear. It was early afternoon, and the sun cast a sienna light over the fields and road on which I walked. There was no traffic—I sang as I walked on a road completely deserted by humans. By the time I reached my destination, dusk had fallen, making the tall firs that flanked the road look like giant soldiers, dark and foreboding, standing watch.

I arrived after dinner in time for dessert, and my visit was brief because I had to take the bus back. Selma walked me to the station and said she was sorry I had not come in time for dinner. Now, whenever I happen to see Selma's photo in my collection, I am reminded of the invitation for "Weinachten," especially that glorious, solitary walk on a sunlit road in my new clothes.

Twenty-five

Bonnie and Frau Kipp disliked Zofie's sister, Marie, from the moment she set foot in the house. Lithe and curvaceous, with jet black hair and large black eyes, she flashed a brilliant smile whenever anyone was around. She walked with a lilt, not unlike an athlete, but there was something more to it, something so feminine that no man failed to notice her.

She did not resemble her sister. Zofie's features were thick, Semitic; Marie's were fine and sensual. Her demeanor was so assimilated into Polish culture that one had a hard time believing her to be anything but a Christian Pole. Her mannerisms and her language did not even hint of anything but that which she claimed to be: a Pole, Catholic, a woman, a very vain woman aware only of herself—and of all men who happened to cross her path.

Marie got the little room that was joined to mine by the open arch, and we became roommates.

Lillie looked at Marie with suspicion and tried her best not to let her enter the shop, which she considered her exclusive province. Lillie's boyfriend, Gunther, often dropped by to visit, and she instinctively knew that she didn't want him to see Marie. Gunther, like many German men, was tall, blond, and in the army, temporarily stationed in Stuttgart. A masculine voice, the uniform, and a keen eye for ladies added charm to his countenance.

At first, Marie kept close to the kitchen, where she made ice cream for the coffeehouse and washed stacks of dishes that were continually being sent down in the dumbwaiter. She helped Francoise keep the kitchen clean. She worked hard because she wanted to make a good impression. With time, however, she began to explore the Kipp territory. She looked for excuses to go to the bakery, where she would ask me something unimportant. Herr Kipp would then stop what he was doing to look at us. She also started delivering various small items directly to the bakeshop and to the coffeehouse when she could have used the dumbwaiter.

It was on one of those brief visits to the bakeshop that she first saw Gunther. I was just unloading a board of bread when she followed me, saying I had dropped one of the loaves. Seeing a man in uniform, she looked him up and down—a look he returned. Lillie saw the contact they made, and her face looked troubled. Since I left the bakeshop after depositing the bread, Marie had no choice but to follow me, but from that day, Marie found reasons to go to the shop, and Gunther's visits became more frequent as well.

Lillie suspected her boyfriend of angling to meet Marie, and when she could stand it no longer, she went to Herr Kipp for help. He ordered Marie not to go to the bakeshop or to the coffeehouse but to use the dumbwaiter instead. She obeyed.

It was not customary for any of us in the Kipp household to go out in the evenings during the workweek. As a precaution against air raids, the city was engulfed in total darkness at night with few conveyances in operation. Cinemas as well as coffeehouses were closed. The air raids made it impossible to enjoy any outing without interruption, especially at night. Yet, none of these hindrances deterred Marie. Several times each week, she went out after her work was finished. No one knew where she went. She often returned at four or five in the morning, passing me wordlessly as I dressed to go down to work   On one of her evenings out, I went to bed early as usual, leaving on the overhead light while I waited for Selma to stop by for a chat. But instead of Selma, in walked Marie with a man, a complete stranger to me. She was in good humor, smiling as she introduced us. He shook my hand, then while making pleasant conversation, he opened a bottle of cologne and flung part of its contents on my featherbed, then followed Marie to her room, where I heard them undress hastily. It was an unsettling night that, unluckily, was not interrupted by an air raid, and since I was unable to sleep, I went down to work before anyone else for the first time since my arrival at the Kipps.

When Herr Kipp and Bonnie came down to the bakery, they found me sitting with the lights on waiting to start the day. I told them that Marie had a guest and that I found it difficult to sleep with an extra person in our room.

That afternoon Marie got a terrible scolding from Frau Kipp, who threatened to fire her if she ever brought another guest to her room. From that day on, Marie treated me with utter contempt, calling me a liar and a thief, and threatened to tell the Kipps that I stole bread to bring to my friends at the factory. I lived in constant fear of what she might do and tried to avoid her as much as possible during the day, but it was difficult at night in the tiny space we both occupied.

She often chose the night to start arguments, waking me from deep sleep to hurl cutting remarks at me, criticizing my behavior unfairly. I did not answer her insults and accusations because I was afraid that anything I might say would exacerbate the outbreak. My only comfort was that she never once mentioned our identity. She was so hysterical during her outbursts that I feared she would stop at nothing to vindicate herself even at the risk of her own safety.

Air raids over Stuttgart were so frequent now that we were being bombed every night, often several times a night, and everyone was short tempered. During the day, after firing the furnace in the basement of the bakery, I sometimes fell asleep as I sat for a moment's rest before going back up. It seemed I fell asleep whenever I sat down until Herr Kipp's voice calling would rouse me.

One night I was in such a deep sleep that even the howl of the sirens did not wake me. Gaston was also late running to the air shelter and instinctively pounded on my door as he passed it. I jumped out of bed and in my nightclothes followed him down. As we raced down the five flights, bombs were already falling—we heard them whistle as they fell through the air and then exploded on impact—knocking us to the floor on each landing.

The factory I visited Sundays was destroyed in an air raid, which ended my visits there. From Maria, Anna, and Jean, who worked in the sanatorium near Heilbronn, I got a letter saying that Weisenhof (the name of the sanatorium) was designated a neutral zone because it was a hospital and was, therefore, exempt from bombardment. An enviable position to be in.

It was becoming clear to all of us that the Germans were losing the war. Newspapers continued to print propaganda of victories on various fronts, but news of costly losses on the Russian front, as the Germans were being pushed back through Poland, filtered through to us from the disabled soldiers who were coming home from field hospitals for discharge.

I overheard furtive conversations between Herr Kipp and Bonnie, expressing fear for the future of Germany, conversations that to me seemed as improbable as they were thrilling. Bonnie now openly regarded me and Marie with reserve, and Marie was no longer criticized for her behavior. Selma, too, seemed to regard me now as the enemy, and I keenly felt the loss of her friendship.

Yet again and again, the Germans rallied, up to the very end of the war, encouraging hope at home, except that the unrelenting air raids that caused us to spend entire days and nights in shelters were bringing a different message.

In Stuttgart, which I gathered had been one of the last cities in Germany to be attacked by air, whole neighborhoods were leveled. Food and shelter were becoming scarce, and masses of people were leaving the city to join relatives in remote parts of the countryside.

The Kipps sent away their children, and that freed Selma from her job. She asked to be allowed to return home, and having no excuse to keep her any longer, they let her go. Despite her impersonal manner toward me of late, I was sad to see Selma leave. She did not know, of course, who I really was, and I could not take the chance to tell her, but I felt that it would probably have made no difference to her whether I was Jewish or Catholic. What did matter to her was that we were on opposite sides of this war and that my side was winning. She had always believed Germany to be invincible. The day she left the Kipps was the last I heard of Selma.

Those of us still left in Stuttgart prepared for the worst. And the worst happened one night as we were all in the air raid shelter, sitting stiffly in chairs placed around the walls.

The noise of the bomb was deafening, and we knew at once that the building had been hit. The shelter remained intact, but the pressure of the falling bomb was apparently so great that some of the elderly people in the shelter died instantly, without as much as a whimper or movement. They simply remained sitting where they had been as if nothing had happened, except they were no longer breathing. White dust covered their hair and shoulders.

None of us from the Kipp household was hurt. The bomb lodged in the marble floor of the entrance lobby, hollowing out most of the interior of the building, but leaving the exterior walls. The standing shell of the building looked like a lacy sculpture on a bed of debris.

Zofie's building was also destroyed that night, and we were brought together in the Arbeitsamt, waiting to be placed again.

Twenty-six

Through correspondence with Jean, Maria, and Anna, we knew that to be assigned to the Weisenhof Tuberculosis Sanatorium would be a wonderful thing, and we began to beg to be sent there, saying that our relatives were already working in the sanatorium and that in these uncertain times, one's relations were the only comfort one has. We pleaded with the clerks at the Arbeitsamt, who would not hear of it at first, but they gave in eventually. When we succeeded, Zofie and I hugged for the second time since meeting in Krakow two years earlier. Zofie's sister, Marie, remained in Stuttgart with a friend. She was not interested in being transferred to Heilbronn.

Weisenhof sat among age-old trees and rolling hills. Acres of lawn and carefully tended flowerbeds surrounded old brick buildings where patients lived. One of those buildings belonged to the staff, and a large dormitory room in the attic, with a row of beds, was given to the five of us: Anna, Maria, Jean, Zofie, and me.

At Weisenhof, I knew for the first time since the war had begun what it was like to live peacefully.

The doctors on the staff there were surprised to have one so young as me sent to work in a sanatorium of a seriously contagious disease. They did not allow administration to place me in a job where I would be directly exposed. I was therefore assigned to the dining hall to serve patients who would soon be discharged. Those patients wore street clothes and were allowed to leave sanatorium grounds. Food was served five times each day: breakfast, second breakfast, dinner, tea, and supper. I did not work alone. Jean and

Anna were fellow waitresses. At Weisenhof, the food was superior and abundant. I put on weight and grew inches. The year I spent there flew.

It was early spring 1945, the day was fine, and I was on break between second breakfast and dinner. Putting my free time to good use, I took a bath and washed my hair. Then, because it was sunny and warm, I decided to dry my hair in the sun. Taking a blanket, I sat with a magazine on an exposed hill near the compound. Suddenly, out of nowhere, I heard the purr of a plane. Spotting it in the distance, I watched as it neared me with such great speed that in seconds it was over me, swooping down in a vertical dive directly over my head, engine screaming. He tore the tops off nearby trees, and I clearly saw the pilot's head. I waved. He turned his head and, with the same suddenness with which he had appeared, lifted off and disappeared into the distance.

I knew that I had just seen a dive bomber, the kind the Americans were using then to target specific areas. I don't know how or why a single plane found itself over Weisenhof. Perhaps it was not even an American plane. I don't remember seeing any markings that would identify it one way or another. At any rate, it was an exciting experience and for days a topic of conjecture among us.

Later on, that same spring, the American Seventh Army liberated us. We remained at Weisenhof, waiting for the end of the war. We continued to work, for which we got food and shelter. We did not disclose our true identities to anyone, not even to the American soldiers who visited us. We were so inculcated with fear that although we knew that we could no longer be harmed for being Jewish, none of us could bring herself to utter the word Jew.

When we all finally traveled back to Stuttgart to a displaced persons (DP) camp under the aegis of UNRA (United Nations Relief and Rehabilitation Agency), it was automatically assumed there that we were Jewish. At that point, we did not deny it. We registered using the same first names we had used in Germany but taking back our family surnames. I kept Eva as my first name since there was no one left to call me Sala, and because I had ceased being Sala on the day I had parted with Mother at the edge of the wood, when I became nameless first and then Eva.

It is not easy to describe the relief we felt as we were gradually gaining back our original identities. It felt perhaps like having been deprived of breath for a long time—air was slowly flowing back into our lungs.

Daily arrivals of survivors from different places, including concentration camps, filled the DP camp. There were survivors from France, Austria, Russia, Poland, and other countries. The mix of so many cultures gave the place a cosmopolitan atmosphere, with activities that included lectures, concerts, and poetry readings by gifted survivors.

I spent one and a half years in that camp waiting for a permanent home. I spent much of my time during the first months looking for my parents and other relatives, a sad search that turned up nothing. I placed my name on a list for emigration to America, knowing that if anyone in my immediate family survived, they would do the same thing.

I remembered the name of my aunt in North Carolina and the name of the town in which she lived. That made it easy to find her, and it helped to speed approval for my emigration. I became eligible in February 1947.

On a cold, snowy day, I sailed on the USS Ernie Pyle, an American Armed Forces ship, with a number of other displaced persons from Bremen Hafen to New York.

My trip to America was long, the weather stormy. Huge waves thrashed the boat, delivering one wallop after another for days on end. It took about ten days to reach New York. Many passengers stayed in their berths, trying to sleep away the time to avoid getting sick. Others hung over the railings of the ship, emptying their stomachs and groaning. I proved to be a good sailor, never skipping a meal and taking it all in stride.

When the announcement was made that we would be in New York the following morning, I was up and ready before dawn, waiting on deck to greet my new country. The day was slow in breaking, and in the distance, a few blinking lights signaled the location of the port. As we neared harbor, there gradually appeared out of the obscurity of the night a body of different shapes, tall and elegant, rising out of the water like a mirage. I was struck by the sheer number of skyscrapers as we moved in slow motion, surrounded by tugboats, in a clear and brilliant dawn.

When the sun rose, it illuminated parts of the buildings where, reflected in window panes, it shot out shards of light, hiding other parts in mauve shadows and giving the whole a look of unreality. Here my life awaits me, I thought. The hellish course behind me, I had earned a passing grade; I knew I could withstand what life had to offer. I felt like a mythological figure emerging from the netherworld to resume life on earth.

The Ernie Pyle rounded the Statue of Liberty, and by now everyone from below was on deck, screaming, crying, laughing, stretching out arms, straining to touch that famous statue. Some stood staring, benumbed. We landed on Ellis Island.

Epilogue

Some years after my arrival in America, I met Zofie, perchance, on a street in New York. She told me that when the war ended, her sister, Marie, looked for and found Frau Kipp living in Stuttgart. Determined to let her at least for a moment taste the kind of fear that we had all felt during the war, and in revenge for the contemptible attitude with which Marie had been treated by Frau Kipp, Marie and two of her friends visited her.

They started by pounding on her apartment door instead of ringing the doorbell. Once inside, they made her crouch in a corner of the room, threatening to beat her into submission if she didn't do as bid. She cried and implored them to let her live, cowering on the floor while they berated her, her people, and her country. She wept and told them that her husband was missing in action. He had been drafted when the total mobilization order had been issued late in 1944, drafting all German males from age sixteen to sixty. She was left alone with her two children. She begged and she wailed. Her hair, which was usually coifed to perfection, was disheveled, and her flashing black eyes were red and swollen. They meant to inflict some physical pain on her and to take her jewelry, but in the end, they could not bring themselves to do any of these things and finally left in disgust.

Zofie was now married, as was her sister, Marie, both living in New York with their husbands. Maria, one of our original group, was living in Virginia with her husband, a chicken farmer. Anna and Jean, who had found her sister in Germany, also came to America because their relatives there claimed them. Anna found her boyfriend from before the war, they married, and both re-entered university in the United States.

I never saw Zofie again after that meeting, but I visited Maria in Virginia and found her to be very happy. Since then, I have had no news, nor have I been in touch with any of the girls from my years in Germany. Perhaps all of us wanted to erase that period of our lives.

Meanwhile I continued inquiries through various sources—organizations, individual survivors from different concentration camps, people who had lived in and around Dabrowa (of whom there were, alas, very few left)—hoping to find a living relative.

What I found follows:

All my many uncles, aunts, and cousins whom I did not mention in this memoir perished in the war.

Uncle Meyer, Father's youngest brother, survived with Ceska and Leon, his children, and remained in Dabrowa, where he eventually married a Christian woman. His first wife and the mother of his children had been murdered. When his current wife left him, he moved to the country and roomed with Mrs. Korona, who was now able to offer him his own bed. He eventually passed away in that lady's home.

Cousin Ceska, my good childhood friend, survived and lives in London with her husband and their three children. Leon moved to Israel, where he fought in the Israeli war of liberation in 1948, for which he received a high army commission for valor.

Aunt Raisa, who had let us use her beautiful apartment in Dabrowa at the beginning of the war when she'd decided to walk with her family to Russia and then to Palestine, made it to Palestine and lived to be eighty-three. She lost her husband to heart failure on that journey. Her children and grandchildren live in Tel-Aviv.

Uncle Emil, Aunt Franka's husband and Father's middle brother, was working in the cleanup crews until 1944 when—his services no longer needed—he was shot together with the others with whom he had worked.

Aunt Franka survived as a Catholic, working for IG Farben in Germany. She arrived in North Carolina in 1948. She lived to be seventy-three.

Uncle Herman was never heard from after he left with Eva in 1942. No one could give me any information about him or about Eva.

Cousin Zela, who had lived near us in Katowice and with whom we later shared Aunt Raisa's apartment in Dabrowa, survived the war and emigrated to Palestine, where she married a Sabra (native Israeli) when she was sixteen years old. She is today a widow, surrounded by her children and grandchildren. Her father had managed to escape to Palestine during the war, and when she arrived there in 1947, they met.

Over the years, I have tried to reminisce with Zela about our childhood. I wanted to know how her mother, my Aunt Gusta, died and what happened to Moniek, her brother who loved the Germans. But she repeatedly denied any knowledge, although she had lived with her mother and brother until the family disintegrated. I don't know if she completely erased all memory of her wartime experiences or if she simply does not want to relive those horrors and refuses to talk about them.

Grandmother was last seen being loaded on the train that was to take her to a concentration camp.

Mother was gassed in Auschwitz.

Father, who lived until the end of the war (as Uncle Meyer recalled it), was then hacked to death with an ax by Christian fellow resistance fighters.

CPSIA information can be obtained at www.ICGtesting.com

229049LV00001B/3/P

9 780966 582765